# SHAKE UP

## SCIENCE 6

**Pearson Education Limited**
Edinburgh Gate
Harlow
Essex CM20 2JE
England
and Associated Companies throughout the
world.

www.pearsonelt.com



First published 2016
ISBN: 978-1-2921-4486-3
**Set in** ArtaStd, AvenirLTPro, BauhausStd,
BradleyHandITCStd, CascadeScriptLTStd,
FuturaLTPro, GillSansInfantStd,
ITCAvantGardeStd, ITCFreemouseCom,
MemphisSRPro, MorrisFreestyleStd,
ReporterLTStd, RuzickaFreehandLTStd,
SpartanLTStd, VAGRoundedLTCYR,
ZapfDingbatsStd, ZemkeHandITCStd
**Printed in** China (CTPSC/01)



**Acknowledgements**
**Picture credits**
The publisher would like to thank the following
for their kind permission to reproduce their
photographs:

(Key: b-bottom; c-centre; l-left; r-right; t-top)

**123RF.com:** 1enchik 59cr, 12tr, 13cr, 13br,
30/2, 30/5, 42/1, 42/3, 46/4, 46/6, 66/3,
66/5, 70/2, 71cr, 72/4, 75/1, 78/6, 87t,
Alhovik 48t, Alzam 48tr, Karina Baumgart
35/3, Roberto Biasini 24tr, 24cr, Blueringmedia
22/1, 22/2, 22/3a, Franck Boston 42/4,
Linda Bucklin 15tr, 17/3, 29br, Leonello Calvetti
20/2, 20/3, 22/5, 22/6, 24c, 82/3, Dunca
Daniel 46/1, Dcylai 69/4, Hadot 36 (c),
Sebastian Kaulitzki 22/4, Galina Khaydukova
35/2, Anna Kukhmar 78/5, Peter Lamb 23tr,
Lightwise 6 (b), Mistac 62/3, Jacek Nowak 63tr,
Steven Prorak 36 (d), Ratmaner 62/2, Nico
Smit 44/4, Martin Spurny 36 (b), Strannikfox
35/4, Sergei Trofimenko 70/5, Yevheniia
Ustinovska 57cr, Russ Witherington 74/2,
Cathy Yeulet 64/3, Worachai Yosthamrong
58/4; **Alamy Images:** National Geographic
Image Collection / Randy Olson 4tl, 82/1,
Sam Toren 6 (a); **Fotolia.com:** 06photo 44/2,
45cr, Giordano Aita 46/5 (right), Alekss
72/2, Anankkml 57tr, Baffineri 5cl, Baibaz
60/4, Bluesnote 62/4, Chalabala 18tr, Johnny
Dao 29cr, Design56 58/1, Destina 46/3,
82/6, Elenathewise 78/3, Floki Fotos 40/5,
Jacek Fulawka 75/3, Graphithèque 40/1,
40/2, 40/3, Herraez 82/2, Highwaystarz
10tr, Illustrez-Vous 69/2, Dr Kateryna 22/8,
Kodamatobi 44/6, Lzf 64/1, Gino Santa
Maria 75/2, Maxsol7 60/3, Jeanne McRight
73tr, Mezzotint 8cl, Molaruso 76/4, Sergii
Mostovyi 35/5, Mariusz Niedzwiedzki 35/1,
OConnor 32tr, Robin2b 41tl, Sergojpg 17/4,
Sondem 30/1, Johan Swanepoel 47c, 47cr,
47b, 48b (background), 49t (background),
50b (background), James Thew 7cr, James
Threw 48tl, Timmary 60/6, Tmass 51tr, 54br,
Toa555 56/2, Viktor 60/5, Tom Wang 38/4,
Xixinxing 68br, Victor Zastol'skiy 65cr, Zentilia
5cr, Zlikovec 62/6, Zurbagan 46/7; **Getty
Images:** John Cancalosi 17/1, Photo-Biotic Leigh
Righton 58/6; **Glow Images:** Image 100. Corbis
64/6; **Imagemore Co., Ltd:** 16br; **Imagestate
Media:** John Foxx Collection 64/4; **Pearson
Education Ltd:** Martyn F Chillmaid 38/2, Mohd
Suhail. Pearson India Education Services Pvt.
Ltd 84cr, Oxford Designers & Illustrators Ltd
22/3b, 22/7; **PhotoDisc:** Tracy Montana /
Photolink 44/1; **PunchStock:** Goodshoot 67cr;
**Shutterstock.com:** 82/4, Anatolich 31br, Cheryl
Ann Quigley 66/1, AP17 74/5, ArTDi101
30/3 (right), Can Balcioglu 59tr, Stephane
Bidouze 36 (e), BlueRingMedia 20/1, Natalia
Bratslavsky 38/1, Eric Broder Van Dyke 58/3,
82/7, Bunnyphoto 74/1, Brian C. Weed 69/6,
C Eng-Wong Photography 36 (a), Leonello
Calvetti 24tl, Cessna152 66/6, Cobalt88
58/2, David Crockett 59tc, Michelle D. Milliman
72/1, Danshutter 74/3, Andrea De Paoli 62/5,
Willy Deganello 70/4, Chris DeRidder 56/6,
Design56 68tl, Shilova Ekaterina 6 (c), El Greco
30/4, Paul Fleet 48tc, 55tr, Glo 70/1, Karen
Grigoryan 70/3, Eric Isselee 73cr, Ivancovlad
64/5, 83/8, Peter J. Wilson 44/5, Sarah Jessup
66/4, Monica Johansen 19cr, K Constantine
66/2, Kichigin 35/6, 54tr, Georgios Kollidas
78/1, Ivan Kuzmin 76/3, Sergey Lavrentev 70tr,
David Lee 67tr, Lepas 56/4, 61tr, Lfstewart 37tr,
Marko Marcello 60/2, Benjamin Marin Rubio
83/9, Oleksiy Mark 45tr, Andrew McDonough
69/1, Dudarev Mikhail 74/4, 87b, Minton
42/2, 54cr, Mopic 78/4, Naluwan 77tr,
Timothy R Nichols 17/6, 18cr, NoPainNoGain
40/6, Ollyy 76/1, Tyler Olson 44/3, Palto
69/3, Belinda Pretorius 38/3, Lee Prince 40/4,
82/5, Pylypenko 17/2, Joshua Resnick 56/3,
Rickyd 69/5, Samarttiw 39cr, 46/2, Oksana
Shufrych 71tr, Siberia 17/5, Maciej Sojka
48cr, 49tr, 50br, Stana 30/6, Stocksnapper
64/2, 72/3, StudioSmart 78/2, Max Topchii
58/5, Evlakhov Valeriy 56/1, Wallenrock
56/5, Yellowj 60/1, Feng Yu 76/2, Sergiy
Zavgorodny 62/1

All other images © Pearson Education

Cover photo © Front: **Getty Images:** laflor r;
**Shutterstock.com:** Ociacia l; Back:
**Shutterstock.com:** 501room l, Belinda Pretorius c,
ssuaphotos r

# Contents

# Unit 1 — Design and function

**1** How does technology help us? Match and write. Also think of your own ideas.

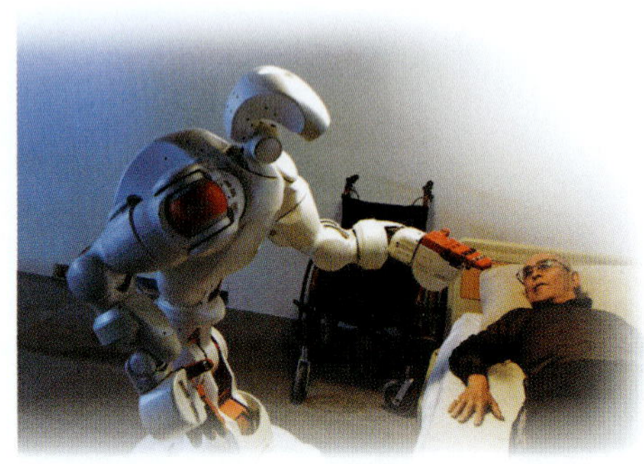

**1** _d_ Technology helps us travel far.

**2** ___ It helps people keep in touch.

**3** ___ It helps us do school research.

**4** ___ It improves the way our bodies work.

**5** ___ Inventions find solutions to problems.

**a** Solar batteries make it possible to use electric machines where there is no electricity.

**b** Doctors can use special machines to help people who have heart problems.

**c** The Internet is a fast source of information.

**d** Trains and airplanes take us from one place to another in very little time.

**e** Cell phones, tablets, and apps help us keep in contact with friends and family.

**2** Unscramble the words. Use the words to complete the sentences.

**1** utcfonin

The ___function___ of an object is the job that it has been designed to do.

**2** ovtneinin

A new ___________ is a product that has been made for the first time.

**3** nisdeg sorpecs

The ___________ ___________ helps us develop new technologies.

**4** pettyroop

A ___________ is the first model of a product that uses new technology.

**3** How do you think computers have changed over the last 30 years? Write.

_______________________________________

**4** Read and write.

> design    invention    technology
> research    ~~solution~~    function
> ~~design process~~

Over the years, the (**1**) _design process_ for developing new computers hasn't changed, but the (**2**) _____________ has. Thirty years ago, computers were not as easy to use as (they) are today because people didn't have the technology we have now. The first computers were very big and slow, and they could not do many things. Design engineers did a lot of (**3**) _____________ to find new technologies to make them better. The results of their research improved the computers' (**4**) _____________ and (**5**) _____________. Computers became smaller and faster and could do a lot more things. Still, there was one big problem that needed a (**6**) _____________. People had to use their computers at home or at work because they needed electricity. The (**7**) _____________ of rechargeable batteries changed all that because now we can take our laptops with us everywhere we go.

**5** Look at **4**. Circle the pronouns. Write the word they replaced.

**1**   _computers_          **2**   _____________

**3**   _____________       **4**   _____________

## Lesson 1 · How does technology mimic living things?

**1** Robotic technology mimics living things. Read and circle.

**1** Which is <u>not</u> a prosthetic limb?

   **a** an artificial arm   **b** an artificial eye   **c** an artificial leg

**2** What does a sensor system do?

   **a** It helps to control movement in robots.

   **b** It makes robots have feelings.

   **c** It does tasks that are too dangerous for people.

**3** What is nanotechnology based on?

   **a** Copying the human body.

   **b** Making everything smaller.

   **c** Moving one atom at a time.

**4** Which is a nanobot?

**a**    **b** 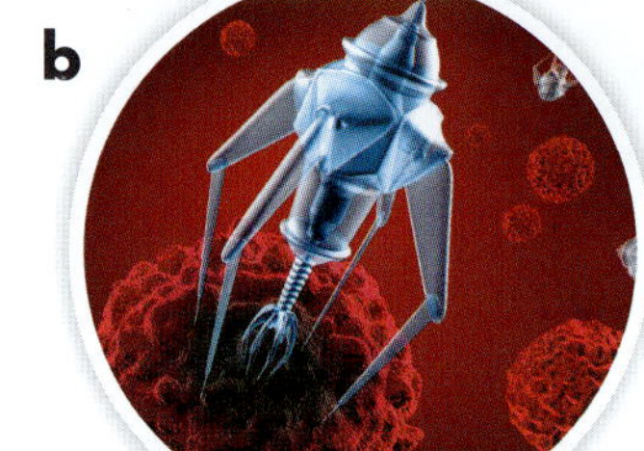   **c** 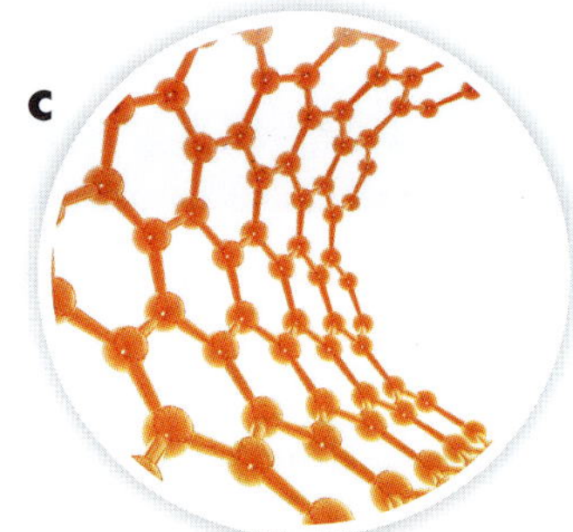

**2** Read and match.

**1** The sensor system in a robot has

**2** Prosthetic limbs can be controlled by

**3** Scientists want to create tiny robots

**4** Some robots are made to mimic

**5** Using nanotechnology, scientists hope to design

**a** called nanobots that can go inside the human body.

**b** machines that are only a few atoms big.

**c** a similar function as the brain and nervous system in the human body.

**d** the muscular and skeletal systems of humans or animals.

**e** electrical signals from the brain.

**3** What do you think the text in **5** is about? Look at the title and picture.

_______________________________________________________________________

**4** Who has superhuman powers? Scan the text in **5** and circle.

**a**  the police detective                     **b**  the scientist

**5** A film review. Read and write.

> atoms    mimic    sensor system    nanotechnology
> prosthetic limbs    ~~nanobots~~

## FILM REVIEW: Super Cop 

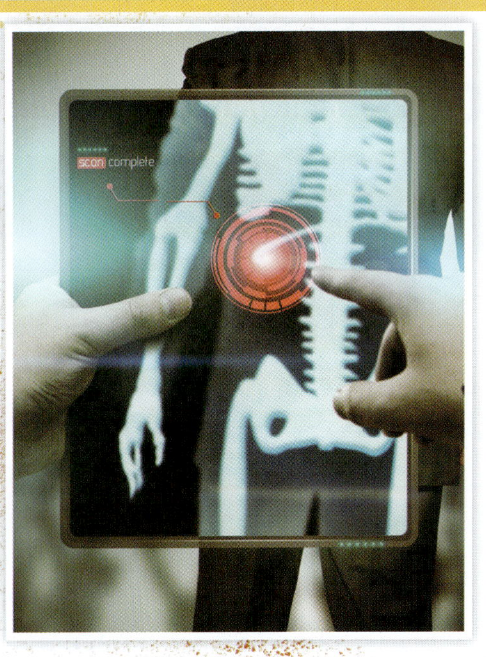


Super Cop is a science fiction film. A scientist wants to make
**(1)** ___nanobots___ that will help sick people. When his best
friend, a police detective, gets injured in a car accident, the
scientist uses **(2)** _______________ to make him well again.
He makes nanobots that are only a few **(3)** _______________
big. These nanobots have a **(4)** _______________ that
helps them group together and change function. They
can **(5)** _______________ any function of the detective's
body, and they give him superhuman powers. He can see
through objects and is very strong. Also, the detective lost
both his legs in the accident. The scientist makes him two
**(6)** _______________ that help him run at 100km per hour!

**6** True or false? Circle *T* (true) or *F* (false).

**1**  The scientist wants to use nanotechnology to help people.              **T** / F

**2**  The nanobots can only do one thing.                                    T / F

**3**  The police detective has superhuman powers because of the nanobots.    T / F

**4**  The police detective has prosthetic legs.                             T / F

**5**  The scientist can run at 100 km per hour.                             T / F

**7** If you could have one superhuman power, what would it be?

_______________________________________________________________________

**8** Underline all the sentences that are joined with *that* in **5** on the previous page.

**9** Read and match.

**1** Robots can have arms and legs     **a** that are sick.

**2** Nanotechnology is a science     **b** that studies how to create very small objects.

**3** Robotic arms can have a sensor system     **c** that helps them swim fast.

**4** Nanobots can help people     **d** that mimic the function of human limbs.

**5** Fish have a skeletal system     **e** that controls the movements of the fingers.

**10** Prosthetic limbs use robotic technology. Write sentences with *that*.

**Grammar Tip**

Some technologies do tasks **that** are too dangerous for people. Airplanes have parts **that** mimic the tails and wings of birds.

**1** These days, there are prosthetic arms and legs. They look like real limbs.

These days, there are prosthetic arms and legs that look like real limbs.

**2** Designers use materials. These materials are very light.

**3** There are a lot of types of prosthetic limbs. They are designed to do different things.

**4** Modern technology has created prosthetic limbs. People can move them with their brains.

**5** Some prosthetic legs have mechanisms. They help people walk and run.

## Lesson 2 · What is the design process?

**1** **People use the design process to develop new technologies. Read and match.**

**1** design process (n)

**2** prototype (n)

**3** plaque (n)

**4** document (v)

**5** ensure (v)

**6** bristles (n)

**7** robotic (adj)

**a** the first model of a product that a designer creates to test if a new technology works

**b** the parts of a toothbrush that clean the teeth

**c** a set of steps for developing new products

**d** to record the details of a process

**e** something that is part of or has to do with a robot

**f** a thin, colorless film that can cover teeth

**g** to make certain

**2** **Read and order from 1–8. Then complete the heading.**

The ______________ process

[ ] **a** Design and construct a prototype.

[ ] **b** Communicate results.

[ 1 ] **c** Do research.

[ ] **d** Choose one solution.

[ ] **e** Identify the problem.

[ ] **f** Evaluate and redesign.

[ ] **g** Test the prototype.

[ ] **h** Develop possible solutions.

**3** Imagine you are an engineer designing a new technology. Complete the answers. Write the missing letters.

**1**  **Q:** _What_ will you do to test if your design works?

   **A:** I'll build a p r o t o t y p e .

**2**  **Q:** How will you remember later what you did at the various stages of the design process?

   **A:** I'll d _ _ _ _ _ _ _ my work.

**3**  **Q:** What will you create to show other people how the parts of your design are put together?

   **A:** I'll create a g _ _ _ _ _ _ organizer.

**4**  **Q:** How will you evaluate how well the prototype works when you test it?

   **A:** I'll take careful m _ _ _ _ _ _ _ _ _ _ _ .

**5**  **Q:** Why will you have to measure everything more than once?

   **A:** To e _ _ _ _ _ that the measurements are c _ _ _ _ _ _ _ .

**4** Look at **3**. Circle the question words.

**5** Write *Who, What, Where, Why,* or *How.*

**1**  **Q:** _____ _Where_ _____ do you test a prototype?

   **A:** In a lab.

**2**  **Q:** ____________ designs new technologies?

   **A:** A design engineer.

**3**  **Q:** ____________ do design engineers need to build a prototype?

   **A:** To ensure that their idea works.

**4**  **Q:** ____________ was the name of the first factory robot?

   **A:** It was called the *Unimate.*

**5**  **Q:** ____________ did the *Unimate* help in the factory?

   **A:** It picked up and stacked hot metal parts.

**6** The design process. Write questions for these answers.

**1 Q:** develop / new technologies?
  _Who develops new technologies?_

  **A:** Design engineers.

**2 Q:** design engineers / use / develop robotic arms?
  _______________________________________________

  **A:** A design process.

**3 Q:** design engineers / sometimes / stop / the development of a prototype?
  _______________________________________________

  **A:** Because the results of the tests are not good.

**4 Q:** design engineers / learn / from testing the prototype?
  _______________________________________________

  **A:** They learn if the new technology works.

**5 Q:** design engineers / communicate / results?
  _______________________________________________

  **A:** They send a report of their invention to groups of people.

**7** A friend has emailed you about new robots that are going to change the way we think about robots. Write six questions to ask your friend about the robots.

> Hi,
>
> Yesterday, I read about some new robots that are made in China. The article was amazing, but also scary! The robots look really odd! They can do amazing things. They will be in the robotics show. Would you like to go and see them?
>
> Bye for now!
>
> Sue

Where _______________________________________________?

Why _______________________________________________?

How _______________________________________________?

What _______________________________________________?

Who _______________________________________________?

When _______________________________________________?

# Unit 2
# Survival and Extinction

## How do animals adapt to survive?

**1** Earth is changing all the time. Read and match.

**1** function (n)

**a** how species' physical characteristics or behaviors change to help them live in their environments

**2** adaptation (n)

**b** what something is designed to do, the reason it is there

**3** survival (n)

**c** a change in physical characteristics or behavior so that a living organism can function better an environment

**4** adapt (v)

**d** what happens to a group of living organisms when they have all died out

**5** extinction (n)

**e** how organisms change so they can live in their environments

**2** Complete the sentences, using the words in 1.

**1** An animal's _adaptation_ has a specific purpose. For example, owls' bigger eyes allow them to see and catch their food more easily.

**2** One ___________ of a duck's webbed feet is to help it swim more easily.

**3** Animals have to ___________ to new conditions to stay alive.

**4** The ___________ of a whole species of animals or plants changes the ecosystem.

**5** The ___________ of a species depends on how well or how fast it can change.

**3** **What is it like to live in the Arctic? Read the text in 4, and think of your own ideas.**

**1** What are the temperature and the climate like?

_________________________________________

**2** What adaptations help animals to survive there?

_________________________________________



**4** **Adaptation in the polar bear. Read and write.**

eat its prey     stop water from going inside     hide from its prey
stored in the fat     insulation against the cold     help it walk

The polar bear has adapted in several ways for survival in the Arctic. The Arctic is very cold and covered with snow. The first thing that a polar bear needs is thick white fur. This adaptation helps the animal in two ways. First, it provides (**1**) _insulation against the cold_, and second, because it is white like the snow, it helps the polar bear (**2**) _________________. Under its fur, there is a thick layer of fat that provides more insulation. The polar bear uses the energy that is (**3**) _________________ when there is no food. Because the polar bear eats meat, it has developed sharp teeth and claws that it uses to catch and (**4**) _________________. The openings of the polar bear's nose can close to (**5**) _________________ when it swims to catch fish for food. Finally, a polar bear's large feet have the same function as snow shoes, to (**6**) _________________ on the snow.

**5** **Adaptation in the camel. Read the table and, in your notebook, write a paragraph about camels.**

| Adaptation | Function |
| --- | --- |
| thick eyebrows | shade the camel's eyes from the sunlight |
| long eyelashes | keep the sand out of the camel's eyes |
| the openings of its nose can close | keep the sand out of the camel's nose |
| hump | stores fat for energy |
| long legs | keep the camel's body away from the hot sand |

# Lesson 1 · How do adaptations help animals?

**1** True or false? Circle *T* (true) or *F* (false). Then correct the false statements.

**1** Plants **migrate** when their habitats change.  T / **F**

*Plants cannot migrate because they cannot move.*

**2** Animals have life cycle **variations** to help them survive in their environment.  T / F

_________________________________________________

**3** Not all the animals of a species develop the same **adaptations**.  T / F

_________________________________________________

**4** Some **extinct species** were unable to adapt to fast changes in their environments.  T / F

_________________________________________________

**5** When a species has new needs, it may develop new physical **characteristics** over time.  T / F

_________________________________________________

**6** **Hibernation** is a state of inactivity when animals try to keep cool in extreme heat.  T / F

_________________________________________________

**7** Some animals do things out of **instinct**, not because someone has taught them.  T / F

_________________________________________________

**2** Animal adaptation. Read and circle the correct answer.

Animal species have to adapt to changes in the environment or they become (**1**) instinct / **extinct**. (**2**) Adaptations / Variations can be both structural and behavioural. Changes happen through the process of natural selection. For example, a long time ago, the members of the lion species that developed a certain (**3**) structural / behavioral adaptation—strong, sharp teeth to help them eat their prey—survived, and passed these adaptations to their young. The animals that didn't have this adaptation didn't survive. Now, all lions have sharp teeth. (**4**) Life cycle variations / Seasonal changes make animals adapt their behavior, too. In winter, woodchuck (**5**) hibernate / migrate to survive the shortage of food. The woodchuck that didn't have this (**6**) instinct / physical characteristic died out. The woodchuck that had this information in their genes survived and passed it on to their young.

**3** **Why did dinosaurs become extinct? Think of your own ideas. Then read and write.**

adaptation    physical characteristics    migrate    extinct
seasonal changes    behavioral adaptation    hibernation

Dinosaurs became **(1)** _____extinct_____ around sixty-five million years ago. We don't know how it happened, but scientists have a few ideas. Here are some of them.

## Volcanoes Changed the Climate

There was a lot of volcanic activity between 63 and 65 million years ago. All these volcanic eruptions changed the climate. **(2)** _____________ to the new climate was not possible because the change happened too fast. Why didn't dinosaurs **(3)** _____________ to another place? Probably because the climate change affected the whole planet.

## Ice Age

The earth goes through an ice age from time to time. Dinosaurs' **(4)** _____________ did not allow them to survive in very cold climates. Some modern animals that are cold-blooded have developed a **(5)** _____________ that helps them survive in the cold—they enter a state like hibernation. **(6)** _____________ wasn't the answer for dinosaurs. They couldn't adapt to such a rapid change in the environment, and they couldn't migrate either!

## An Asteroid Hit the Earth

Many scientists think that an asteroid damaged the atmosphere, made sunlight disappear, and changed the climate. **(7)** _____________ stopped, and there was just a very long, cold, dark winter. Many plants died. This affected the food chain, and dinosaurs died because they had no food. It sounds possible to me!

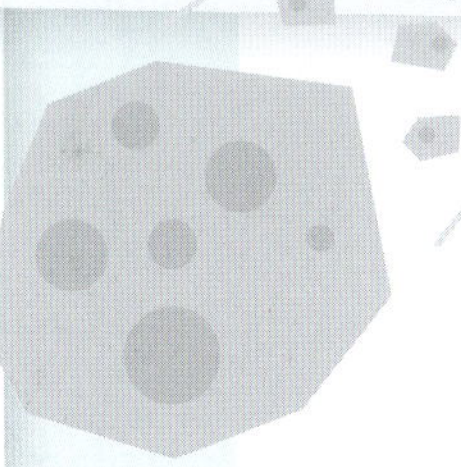

**4** **Look at 3. Circle the correct answer.**

**1**  One explanation for why dinosaurs died is that they couldn't _____________.
  **a**  move fast
  **b**  adapt to the climate changes

**2**  The dinosaurs couldn't survive in a cold climate because they didn't have _____________.
  **a**  the right body temperature
  **b**  the instinct to hibernate

**3**  There were no seasonal changes because _____________.
  **a**  there was no sunlight
  **b**  the plants died

**5** **How do animals adapt? Read and match.**

**1** If an owl cannot see well,

**2** When the weather is warm,

**3** If there is a food shortage,

**4** When a predator approaches it,

**5** If a change happens over a long period of time,

**6** When a lion cub pounces on its mother's tail,

**a** the blue-ringed octopus turns yellow with blue rings.

**b** species can adapt to it.

**c** baby birds can survive better.

**d** it learns how to pounce on its prey.

**e** it cannot catch its prey.

**f** animals may move to other places.

**6** **Zebras' behavioral adaptations help them avoid their predators. Write sentences, using *when* or *if* and the correct form of the verbs.**

> **Grammar Tip**
>
> A species cannot survive **if** it does not adapt to changes.
> **When** animals hibernate, they become inactive to conserve energy.

**1** zebras / stand / close to one another / a lion / cannot attack / them
   *If zebras stand close to one another, a lion cannot attack them.*

**2** a lion / can't see / one animal / there / be / lots of stripes together
   _______________________________________________

**3** zebras / cross / a river / they / have to / look out for / alligators
   _______________________________________________

**4** zebras / move / fast enough / the alligators / not catch / them
   _______________________________________________

**5** a predator / try / to go / near / zebras / they / hear / it / from a distance / and / run away
   _______________________________________________
   _______________________________________________

**1** **What is it? Match and write.**

> palaeontologist   fossil   ~~hadrosaur~~   coal   sauropod   oil

1 ___hadrosaur___

2 ____________

3 ____________

4 ____________

5 ____________

6 ____________

**2** **Match the words from 1 with the descriptions. Write.**

**1** They are fossil fuels.  ___coal, oil___

**2** They are extinct.  ____________

**3** They study the fossils of plants, animals, and other organisms.  ____________

**4** The purpose of one of their physical characteristics may have been to attract mates.  ____________

**5** They had small heads, long necks, and enormous bodies.  ____________

**6** They can tell us what extinct organisms looked like.  ____________

**7** We use them to produce electricity.  ____________

**3** **What clues do you think a fossil can give us about the plant or animal it comes from and its environment?**

_______________________________________________

**4** **Read the text in 5. Think and circle.**

**1** Who wrote the text?

  **a** A science teacher

  **b** A palaeontologist

  **c** A student

**2** What type of text is it?

  **a** A science textbook

  **b** An essay

  **c** A scientific study



The kind of language used in a written text can give you clues about who wrote it, and why.

**5** **What does a paleontologist do? Read and write.**

> fossil fuels    fossils    organisms
> palaeontologists    remains    sauropods

I'd love to understand more about the history of life on Earth, so I would like to become a (**1**) _paleontologist_. Some people think that (**2**) _______________ only study dinosaurs. Well, it is one of the things they do, but the science of paleontology is mostly about studying (**3**) _______________.

(**4**) _______________ tell us about (**5**) _______________ (animals, plants, fungi, bacteria, and other living things) that lived in the past. They are mostly extinct species now, so we can only find out things about them by studying their (**6**) _______________.

(**7**) _______________ work a lot like detectives: they study clues. From these clues they can guess what a plant or animal looked like, what it ate, or where it lived. For example, by looking at the teeth of (**8**) _______________, we know that they were vegetarians.

(**9**) _______________ can even tell us what Earth looked like millions of years ago. Some plant fossils are found in deserts. This tells us that some deserts have changed and rivers used to run through them. When sea animal fossils are discovered on mountains, we learn that in the past these places used to be under the sea. By studying where a fossil is found and by doing some tests, (**10**) _______________ can tell when a plant or animal lived. This helps us form an idea of how life on Earth has developed over millions of years.

What I find amazing is how matter is recycled on our planet. What do I mean? Think about (**11**) _______________ like coal and oil that we use in power plants and to run our cars. They are made from (**12**) _______________ that lived many millions of years ago!

**6** **Facts about fossils. Circle the correct words.**

**1** The timeline of the history of Earth **calls** / **is called** the Geologic Time Scale.

**2** Some modern animals **relate** / **are related** to dinosaurs.

**3** Paleontologists **compare** / **are compared** plant fossils with modern plants that look like them.

**4** Many fossils **find** / **are found** within layers of rock.

**5** Plants and animals **change** / **are changed** slowly over time.

**6** Some areas that **cover** / **are covered** with water used to be dry land millions of years ago.

> **Grammar Tip**
>
> A scientist who studies fossils **is called** a paleontologist. Fossil fuels **are used** to produce electricity.

**7** **Rewrite these sentences as passive sentences. Don't use the underlined words.**

**1** We find fossils everywhere.
   *Fossils are found everywhere.*

**2** Scientists make new discoveries every day.

**3** They compare hadrosaurs to some modern birds.

**4** Power plants produce electricity from coal.

**5** Machines turn oil into energy.

**6** We consume less electricity to conserve fossil fuels.

**7** Scientists discovered fossils of giant sea turtles in South Dakota.

# Body Systems and Function

**How does my body work?**

**1** There are three systems in our bodies. Look at the pictures and write the missing letters.

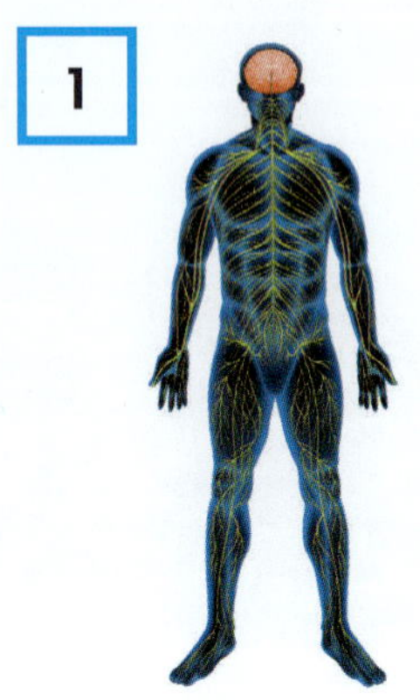

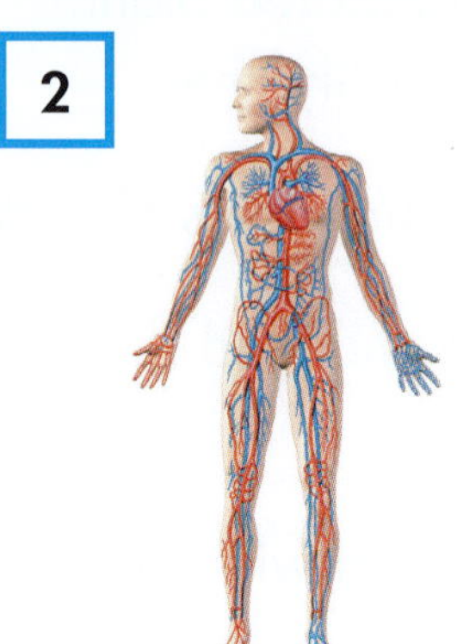

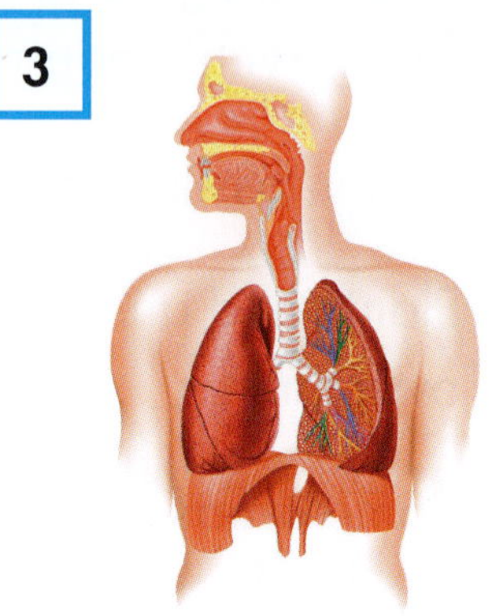

**1** 1 __ __ r __ __ u __  system

**2** 2 c i __ c __ __ __ t o __ y  system

**3** 3 r __ __ p i __ a t __ r y  system

**2** What are their functions? Look at the pictures in **1**. Match and write.

**a** It controls our movements, our thinking, and what we feel with our body.

**b** It helps our body breathe air in and out.

**c** It pumps blood around our body.

**3** Which body system is working? Read, think and match. Explain what is happening.

**a** I'm climbing the stairs, and I'm out of breath. `1` `3`

_I am inhaling oxygen and my heart is pumping it around my body._

**b** I'm blowing out the candles on my birthday cake.

**c** I've stopped running. My heart is beating very fast.

**4** **How can you keep your body healthy? Write.**

_______________________________________________

**5** **This website gives advice on staying healthy. Read and underline the main points of advice.**



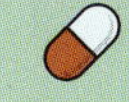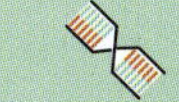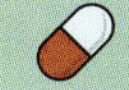

Your respiratory system is constantly attacked by viruses and bacteria. There are steps you can take to avoid catching or spreading them, like staying away from sick people and keeping your immune system healthy and strong. If you're already sick, stay at home for a few days. When you're with other people, try to avoid spreading the virus. Cover your nose and mouth with a tissue when you sneeze.

Exercise makes your lungs stronger and helps them work better. Sports are a fun way of exercising, so joining an afterschool sports club is a good idea. Tobacco smoke is one of the worst things for your health in general, and especially for your lungs, so stay away from places where people smoke.

**6** **Look at the text in 5. Circle _T_ (true) or _F_ (false).**

**1** There's nothing you can do to avoid getting a respiratory illness. T / **(F)**

**2** Doing sports helps the function of your lungs. T / F

**3** Tobacco smoke is only dangerous for people who smoke. T / F

**7** **How can you keep your nervous system working well? Write some advice.**

1 exercise / body and brain: do activities / make you / use your brain, e.g., word or number puzzles
_Exercise your body and your brain. Do activities to make you use your brain, like word or number puzzles._

2 eat / right foods: foods / rich in minerals / vitamins B1 and B12 / as well as / healthy fats / in nuts and fish
___________________________________________

3 drink / water: helps / functions / of your brain / without water / tired / 6–8 cups a day
___________________________________________

4 sleep / well: helps / functions / of your memory / sleep / 10–11 hours a day
___________________________________________

## Lesson 1 · What is the circulatory system?

**1** The circulatory system. Unscramble the letters and write the words.

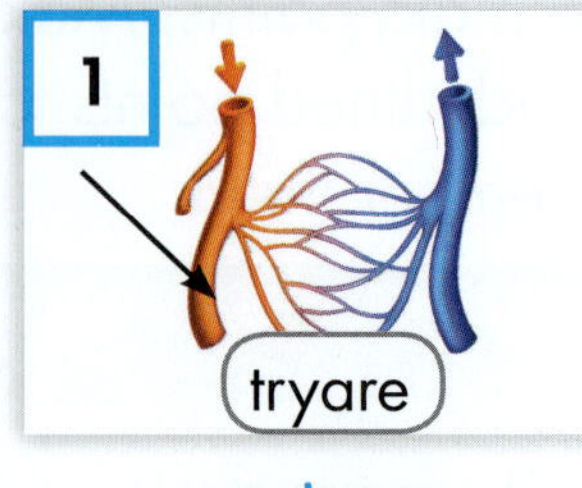


_artery_

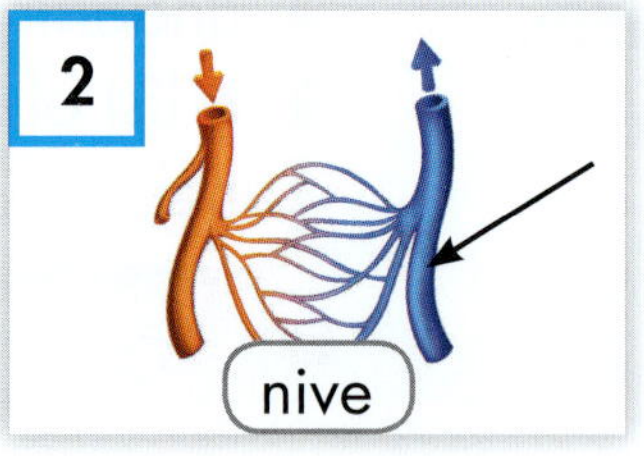


_______________

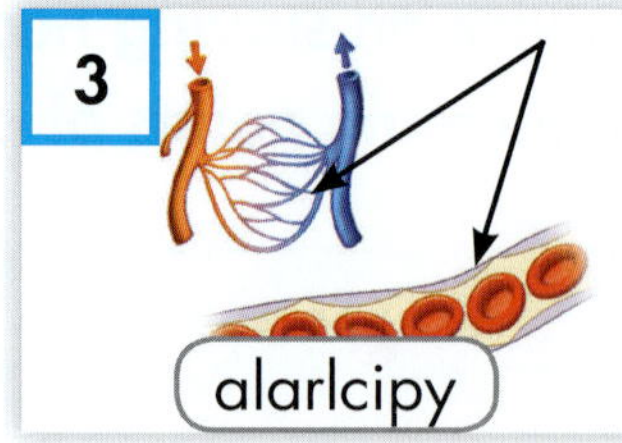


_______________

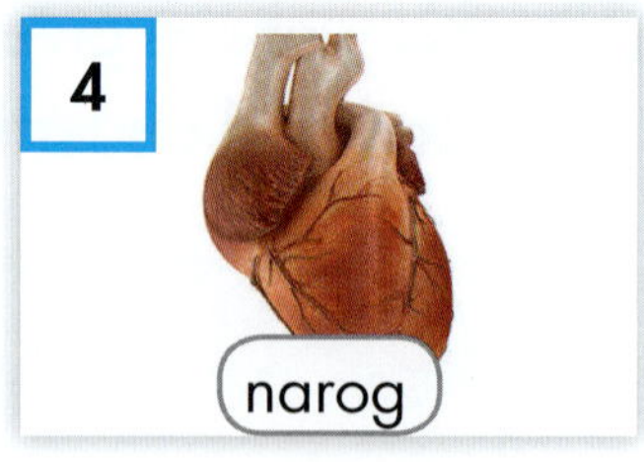


_______________

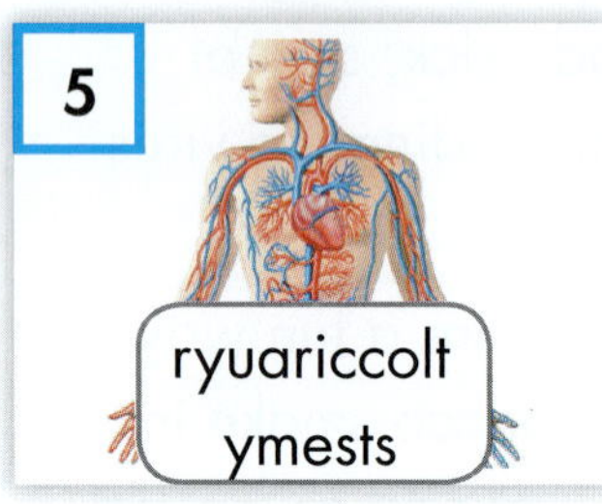


_______________

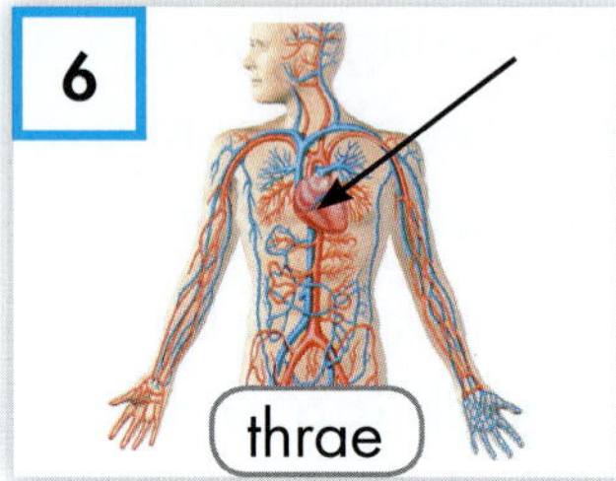


_______________

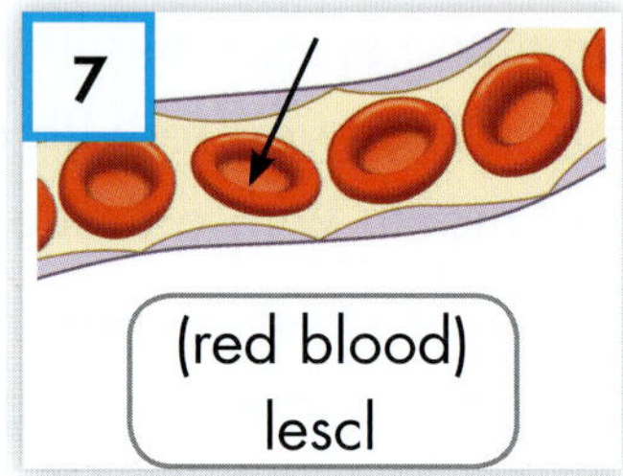


_______________

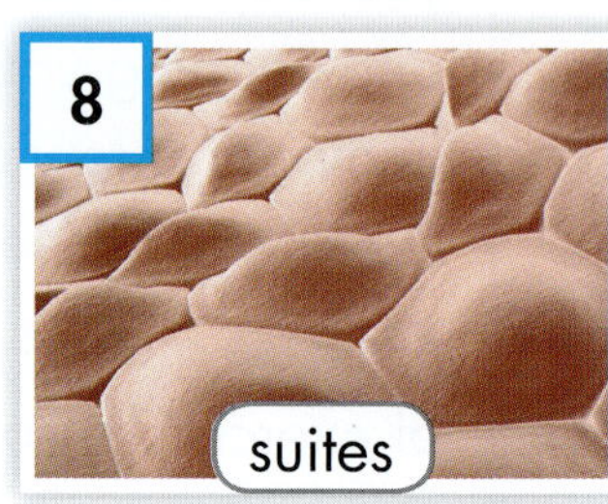


_______________

**2** What is it? Read the definitions, find the words in **1**, and write.

**1** _______________ A group of different tissues that join and work together to do one main job in the body.

**2** _______________ The basic unit that builds an organism. There are organisms that have only one of them and organisms that can have trillions of them.

**3** _______________ A group of the same kind of cells that work together to do the same job.

**3** Facts about the circulatory system. Mark (✓) the correct sentences. Correct the other sentences.

Veins                                    arteries
**1** ~~Arteries~~ carry blood toward the heart, and ~~veins~~ carry blood away from the heart.

**2** Veins have valves to keep blood moving in one direction only. ✓

**3** The circulatory system includes the heart, blood, lungs, and blood vessels.

**4** The blood takes in oxygen and gets rid of carbon dioxide in the heart.

**5** The heart is a system.

**6** A system is a set of things that work together as a whole.

**4** **How does blood move through the body? Read and write.**

ventricle    ~~lungs~~    cells    atrium    organs    system    veins    artery

The two most important functions of the (**1**) ___lungs___ are breathing in oxygen, which can be carried to the body's cells, and waste removal, which means getting rid of carbon dioxide from the body. The circulatory (**2**) ______________ has many functions: it carries nutrients to the smallest living units of our body, the (**3**) ______________; it helps the body keep a steady temperature; and it protects the body from disease.

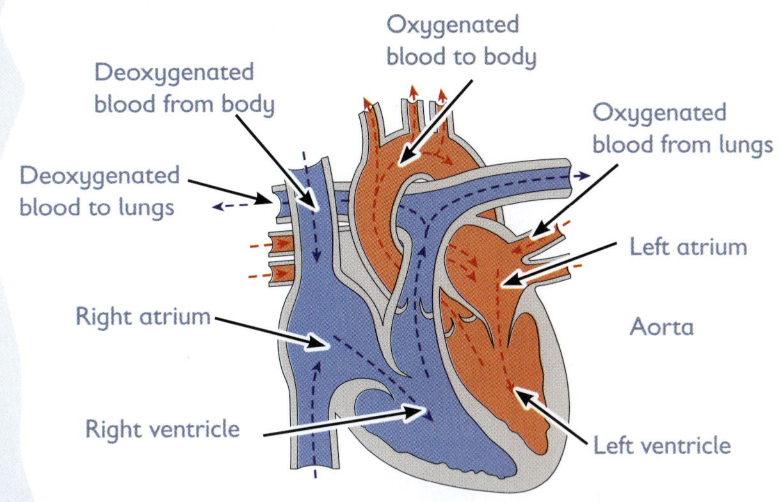


The circulatory system works together with the most important (**4**) ______________ of the respiratory system, the lungs, to help clean and oxygenate the blood. Deoxygenated blood (blood that has lost its oxygen) leaves the right (**5**) ______________ of the heart. An (**6**) ______________ takes this blood to the lungs. In the lungs, the blood gets rid of the carbon dioxide and replaces it with oxygen. The oxygenated blood travels back to the heart through (**7**) ______________ that connect the lungs with the heart. It collects into the left (**8**) ______________. From there it is pumped into the left ventricle, ready to start its journey back around the body.

**Grammar Tip**

**Larger** organisms are made of trillions of cells.
**The smallest** arteries branch to become capillaries.

**5** **Read the text in 4 again. In your notebook, write the functions of the circulatory system.**

**6** **Read and write true sentences to compare the items. Use *than* for 1–3, and *the* for 4–5.**

**1** tissue — organ   small      _A tissue is smaller than an organ._

**2** vein — capillary   big      ______________________________

**3** vein — artery   have / thin walls      ______________________________

**4** organ — cell — tissue   small      ______________________________

**5** aorta — regular artery — veins   big      ______________________________

# Lesson 2 · What is the respiratory system?

**1** The respiratory system helps you breathe. Match and write.

exhale    bronchioles    diaphragm    inhale    air sacs    trachea    lung

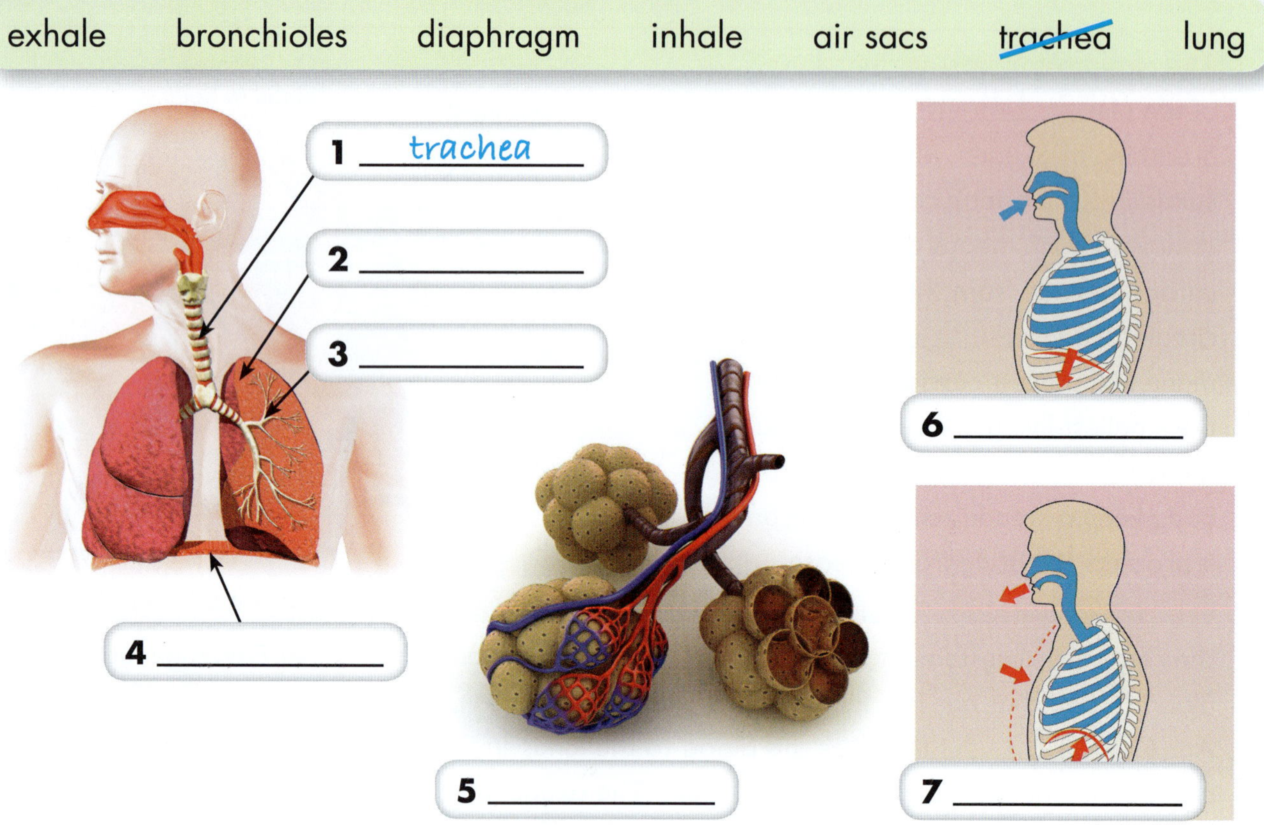


**2** Read and complete, using the words from 1.

**Q:** What happens every time we breathe in and out?

**A:** To breathe in, or (**1**) _____inhale_____, and to breathe out, or (**2**) ______________, we need to use our (**3**) ______________ system. First of all, our brain tells our body that we need oxygen. When we inhale, sets of tubes help the air travel through our body, and the air enters our nasal cavities. The air then passes through the larynx and the (**4**) ______________ on its way to the (**5**) ______________. From there air goes into the bronchi. The bronchi branch out into smaller tubes like a tree. At the end of the branches, we find the smallest tubes of all, called (**6**) ______________. These tubes end in clusters of tiny (**7**) ______________. This is where our blood takes in oxygen and lets out carbon dioxide. When that's done, our brain tells our body to get rid of the carbon dioxide. That air leaves our body through the same tubes that helped fresh air get in. As we (**8**) ______________, the carbon dioxide leaves our body.

**3** **How does the respiratory system help you sing? Read and circle the best option.**



When you read texts with advice or instructions, look for the logical connections between the individual steps.

### How to control your breathing

When you sing, your respiratory system does its job as usual. The difference is that you control how the air goes in and out.

**Breathe in**

1  Keep your back straight and your shoulders relaxed. It helps you have full control of your respiratory system.

2  (**1**) Inhale / **Exhale** in exactly the same way as you normally do.

3  Take in as much air as you need to feel comfortable.

4  Let your (**2**) **trachea** / **diaphragm** move as far down as it can without you pushing it.

5  Let air fill your (**3**) **lungs** / **air sacs**.

**Breathe out**

1  Start singing as you (**4**) **exhale** / **inhale**.

2  Use your rib muscles to keep your rib cage up and out, so that your (**5**) **bronchioles** / **lungs** are full of air. Don't move your ribcage.

3  Push your (**6**) **diaphragm** / **lungs** up slowly. You will be doing this right when you do it without thinking about it.

4  Send only a little air to your vocal cords. Try not to use more air than when you speak. If you push your (**7**) **lungs** / **diaphragm** to send more air than necessary, your vocal cords work harder and you don't get a good result.

**4** **Imagine you have a test in a few days, and you're feeling stressed. Read the email from a friend and do the breathing exercise. Does it work? Think about these questions.**

**Before the Exercise:** How are you feeling? In what way do you expect the breathing exercise to help you? _______________________________________

**During the Exercise:** Are you following the steps of the exercise correctly? _____________

**After the Exercise:** What effect has the exercise had on how you are feeling? Has it helped? Will you do it again? _______________________________________

Hi! Here is a breathing exercise that helps me when I'm stressed:

Place one hand on your tummy and one hand on your chest. Count to six as you inhale. Make sure your diaphragm moves down, not your chest. Count to eight as you exhale. Make sure your diaphragm moves up. Do the exercise for five minutes. I hope it helps!

## Lesson 3 · What is the nervous system?

**1** **The nervous system controls your reactions to the environment. Unscramble the letters. Read and write.**

**1** senuovr eytmss _________________

Your __nervous system__ collects information about what is happening inside and outside your body.

**2** nsese gronsa _________________

Your _________________ react to changes in the environment and inform your brain.

**3** evsner _________________

Your nervous system uses _________________ to send and receive information throughout your body.

**4** onneru _________________

A _________________ is the smallest part of your nervous system.

**5** pasinl orcd _________________

The _________________ communicates with your brain to send and receive messages.

**6** rbian _________________

Some involuntary actions are not controlled by the _________________.

**2** **Facts about the nervous system. Circle the correct words.**

**1** Your mouth, ears, nose, tongue, and skin are your **nervous** / **sense** organs.

**2** Your eyes have parts that sense light, and they inform the spinal **cord** / **brain**.

**3** You ears respond to sound waves. They also help you control your **balance** / **nerves**.

**4** Your nose responds to chemicals in odors, and uses the **brain** / **neurons** to send signals.

**5** The taste **neurons** / **buds** in your tongue detect if something tastes sweet or salty.

**6** Messages about changes in temperature are sent to the brain by the **nerves** / **senses** in the skin.

**3** **Write present passive sentences. Use the underlined words and *by*.**

**1** <u>The sense organs</u> send signals to the brain.

  <u>Signals are sent to the brain by the sense organs.</u>

**2** <u>The nervous system</u> collects information about the environment.

  ______________________________________________

**3** <u>The dendrites</u> receive information from other neurons.

  ______________________________________________

**4** <u>The cerebrum</u> takes up the largest part of your brain.

  ______________________________________________

> **Grammar Tip**
>
> Signals from your sense organs **are read by** the brain. Your spinal cord **is protected by** your backbone.

**4** **What do your sense organs do during these activities? What does your nervous system do? How does your brain react? Complete the chart.**

| | Playing a Computer Game | Eating a Sandwich | Riding a Bike |
|---|---|---|---|
| **Nose** | | It senses the chemicals in the odors and sends signals to the brain about how the sandwich smells. | |
| **Ears** | They sense sound waves and send signals to the brain about the game sounds. | | They sense (**1**) ______ sound waves ______ and (**2**) __________________. They help you control (**3**) __________. |
| **Eyes** | (**4**) ______________________ | (**5**) ______________________ | (**6**) ______________________ |

# Review 1–3

**1** Do the quiz. Circle *a*, *b*, or *c*.

**1** Robotic __ has created prosthetic limbs that function much like real limbs.

**a** control     **b** technology     **c** signals

**2** Robots have a __ system and a computer to control movement.

**a** sensor     **b** nervous     **c** brain

**3** Engineers use the design __ to develop products and processes that solve problems.

**a** diagram     **b** process     **c** solution

**4** __ come from the remains of organisms that lived millions of years ago.

**a** Dinosaurs     **b** Modern organisms     **c** Fossil fuels

**5** Species adapt to slow changes in their environment by developing new __.

**a** physical characteristics     **b** extinct species     **c** survival purposes

**6** __ adaptations in animals are passed from the parents to their young.

**a** Instinct     **b** Learned     **c** Behavioral

**7** The heart belongs to the __ system.

**a** respiratory     **b** circulatory     **c** nervous

**8** Oxygen enters the blood through the __ in the lungs.

**a** bronchi     **b** air sacs     **c** dendrites

**9** When we __, carbon dioxide leaves the body.

**a** relax     **b** inhale     **c** exhale

**10** The __ is protected by the backbone.

**a** spinal cord     **b** brain     **c** nose

You get one point for each correct answer. What's your score?

**1–3** Oh dear!   **4–5** OK.   **6–8** Very good!   **9–10** Excellent!

**2** **Do the crossword puzzle.**

**Across →**

**2** Design engineers build a _____________ to test their solution.

**5** The eyes, heart, lungs are _____________.

**7** The design process solves these.

**8** Robotic arms are designed to _____________ the movement of human arms.

**10** The smallest tube that carries blood.

**Down ↓**

**1** These changes to the environment happen four times a year.

**3** Part of the body that is bigger than a cell, and smaller than an organ.

**4** The dodo is _____________. There are none left alive.

**6** Part of your heart. It collects blood and pushes it into the ventricle.

**9** A fossil fuel.

**Joke time!**

**Q:** Can you name ten dinosaurs in ten seconds?

**A:** Yes, I can—five sauropods and five hadrosaurs.

#  Water and Weather

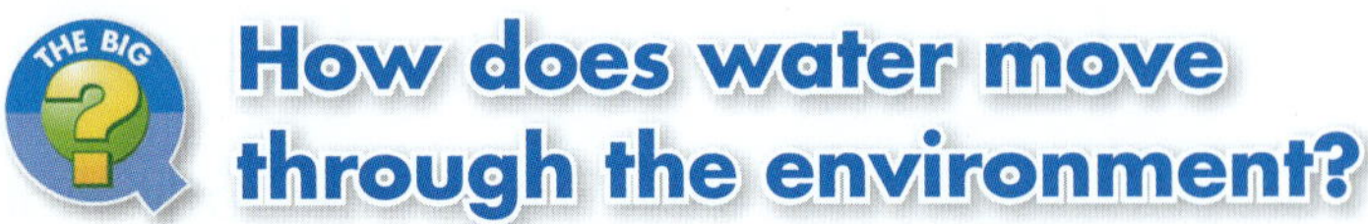

**How does water move through the environment?**

**1** **Weather. Unscramble the letters and write the words.**

**1** peractitipoin

_precipitation_

**2** tehomemterr

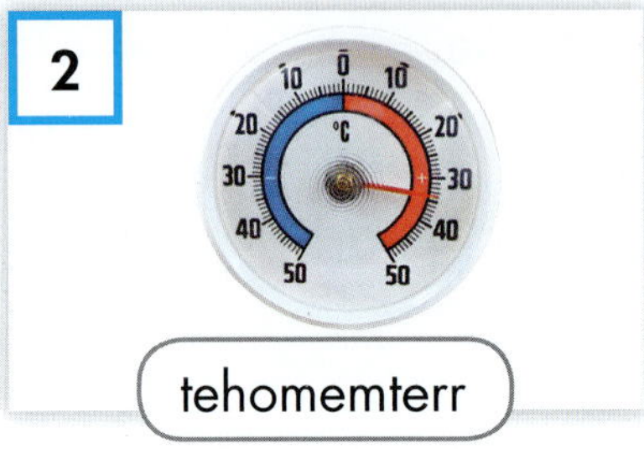

**3** siruetom

**4** ria rpsueres

**5** iwdn peesd

**6** oswn

**2** **What is it? Read the definitions, find the words in 1, and write.**

**1** _Air pressure_ is the force of air as it presses down on an area.

**2** A _____________ is a tool that measures air temperature.

**3** _____________ is frozen water droplets that fall from the sky and cover the ground.

**4** _____________ is water that is present in the air but that we cannot always see.

**5** _____________ is how fast the wind moves.

**6** _____________ is rain, snow, sleet, or hail that falls from the clouds to the ground.

**3** **Have you ever seen sleet, snow, or hail? Write about what they looked and felt like.**

_____________________________________________

_____________________________________________

**4** How do you think people predicted the weather before they had the technology to do it?

_______________________________________________

**5** Read and match the headings to the paragraphs.
Write 1, 2, 3, or 4. There is one extra heading.

**1** Why Technology Doesn't Work for Weather Prediction

**2** Predicting the Weather Without the Use of Technology

**3** Why People Need Weather Forecasts

**4** Technology and Weather Prediction



Each paragraph in a text has a different thing to say about the topic.

### Predicting the Weather by Anna Banks

**A** _______________

Weather forecasts tell us what the weather is going to be like in the next few days. For some people, this is very important. Farmers need to plan their work around precipitation. Rain is good in general, but snow isn't because it can damage plants. Sea travelers need to know wind speeds. It makes all the difference between a smooth and an unsafe trip.

**B** _______________

In the past, when there was no technology to help, people tried to use the sky and the behavior of animals to help them predict the weather. For example, birds flying high in the sky meant good weather would continue. People also used their senses. For example, if you could smell the soil in the air, a lot of moisture was coming soon.

**C** _______________

Modern technology helps make weather forecasts more accurate. Scientists collect and study information about the weather, and use special methods to make their predictions. But, even with the use of technology, we can never be 100% sure.

**6** Counting the sounds that crickets make can help you estimate the temperature. Read and answer the question.

**1** Count the number of chirps a cricket makes in 25 seconds.

**2** Divide this number by three. Then add four.

**3** The number you find is an estimate of the outside temperature in degrees Celsius.

**If you count 96 chirps, what's the temperature?** _______________

**1** Scientists called meteorologists study the weather. Read and mark (✓).

**1** What two things do we NOT need to know to describe the weather?

- [ ] temperature
- [✓] moon phase
- [ ] wind speed
- [ ] wind direction
- [ ] air pressure
- [ ] water pressure
- [ ] moisture in the air
- [ ] season
- [ ] precipitation

**2** What does a meteorologist NOT do?

- [ ] collect data
- [ ] predict the weather
- [ ] plan agricultural activities
- [ ] study the weather

**2** The blanket of air that surrounds Earth is its atmosphere. Read and match.

**1** Humidity

**2** The equator

**3** Barometric pressure

**4** Circulation

**a** is the pushing force of the atmosphere.

**b** is the amount of water vapor in the air.

**c** is the movement of air that redistributes heat.

**d** is the imaginary line that divides Earth into the Northern Hemisphere and the Southern Hemisphere.

**3** Winds follow patterns over continents. Read and write.

trade     jet stream

**1** A polar _____________ is a narrow band of high speed wind that blows from west to east over North America.

**2** _____________ winds blow almost constantly near the equator.

**4** How do you think the difference in air pressure creates a wind? If the difference is bigger, will the wind be stronger? _______________________________________

_______________________________________________________________________________

**5** Read and write. Were your ideas in **4** correct?

> circulation    atmosphere    weather    humidity
> ~~meteorologists~~    barometric pressure

### Weather Forecasting Made Easy

When you watch the weather forecast on TV, do you sometimes think that the **(1)** _meteorologists_ who give them speak a language of their own? High and low pressure systems, levels of humidity, and percentages of precipitation: what a lot of confusing words! Let's try to explain them.

High and low pressure systems have to do with **(2)** _______________. What you need to know is that a high pressure system is a mass of cool dry air that generally brings good weather, clear skies, and low-speed winds. On a **(3)** _______________ map, it is represented by an *H*. A low pressure system is represented by an *L*. It's a mass of warm, moist air that generally brings clouds, rain or snow, and strong winds. Wind is a result of the difference in temperature and air pressure between places that allows the **(4)** _______________ of air. The bigger the difference in pressure and temperature, the stronger the wind. The **(5)** _______________ in low pressure systems can make us feel the heat and cold more. When it's hot and humid, we feel a lot more uncomfortable than when it's hot and dry. This is because the moisture in the **(6)** _______________ doesn't allow much water to evaporate from our bodies to cool us down. →

**6** Read the text in **5** again, and correct the sentences.

**1** ~~Newscasters~~ give the weather forecast on TV.  _Meteorologists_

**2** A high pressure system means there's going to be rain and snow.  _______________

**3** Differences in levels of humidity create strong winds.  _______________

**4** Humidity makes the weather hotter or colder.  _______________

**5** We feel hotter when water evaporates from our bodies.  _______________

**7** Different types of winds affect the weather in different ways. Read and write one or two words.

(**1**) ______________, which are narrow bands of high-speed wind, can affect local weather. (**2**) ______________, however, which are more persistent patterns of wind, blow near the warmest part of our planet, the (**3**) ______________.

**8** What are the past participles of these verbs? Read and write.

| been | blown | gone | become |
|---|---|---|---|
| seen | had | fallen | made |



| | Verb | Past participle | | | Verb | Past participle |
|---|---|---|---|---|---|---|
| **1** | have | had | | **5** | be | ______________ |
| **2** | go | ______________ | | **6** | fall | ______________ |
| **3** | see | ______________ | | **7** | become | ______________ |
| **4** | make | ______________ | | **8** | blow | ______________ |

**9** Write questions with *Have you ever...* Then answer for you.

**1** Q: _Have you ever seen snow?_ see / snow
   A: _Yes, I have._

**2** Q: ______________________________ be / in a storm
   A: ______________

**3** Q: ______________________________ use / a barometer
   A: ______________

**4** Q: ______________________________ make / a weather forecast
   A: ______________

**5** Q: ______________________________ travel / to the equator
   A: ______________

**10** Write about the weather in your area today. Think about temperature, humidity, air pressure, and winds. Then write a weather forecast for tomorrow.

**1** **What are clouds and precipitation made of? Read and write.**

hail    water droplets    altitude    snowflake    sleet    ice crystals

altitude

**2** **Air temperature affects clouds and precipitation. Read and write the words from 1.**

**From the Sky to the Ground: the Journey of Water Through Air**

At some (**1**) _altitudes_, and depending on the temperature, ice crystals or tiny water droplets form clouds. (**2**) ______________ join together and grow larger until they become snowflakes. (**3**) ______________ join together and become larger. When they become too heavy, they begin falling through the air as rain. If the temperature is 0 °C or lower, ice crystals fall to the ground as (**4**) ______________. If the temperature is warmer than 0 °C, snowflakes become water droplets, and fall as rain. If the temperature drops below 0 °C as rain falls, it becomes (**5**) ______________. If there's a thunderstorm and rain is blown back through the icy clouds, it becomes (**6**) ______________.

**3** **What types of cloud can you see? Read and match.**

**1** **Altocumulus** clouds look like small, puffy balls. They usually form between 2 km and 7 km above the ground. __c__

**2** **Fog** is a type of cloud at ground level. It forms when the cool air near the ground makes water condense into tiny droplets. _____

**3** **Cumulonimbus** clouds grow vertically. Their base can be as low as 1km above the ground and their top as high as 12 km. They can cause thunderstorms. _____

**4** **Stratus** clouds are low-level clouds that can cover the whole sky. They are often seen less than 2 km above the ground. _____

**5** **Cirrus** clouds are thin, wispy, white, high-level clouds. They form more than 6 km above the ground. _____

**4** **How high are clouds? Look at 3. Complete.**

| High-altitude clouds (higher than 6 km): | Clouds between 1 km and 12 km above ground: |
|---|---|
| **1** _____cirrus_____ | **5** _____________ |
| Mid-altitude clouds (between 2 km and 7 km): | |
| **2** _____________ | |
| Low-altitude clouds (lower than 2 km): | |
| **3** _____________ **4** _____________ | |

**5** **Look at 3. Answer the questions.**

**1** Which clouds are "rain clouds"? _______________________________________

**2** Which clouds are closest to the surface of Earth? _______________________

**3** Which clouds can hide most or all blue sky? ___________________________

**6** **Clouds and precipitation. Read and write.**

**1** If it ___rains___ (*rain*) in a very hot and dry place, the water ___will evaporate___ (*evaporate*) before it reaches the ground.

**2** If you ___________ (*see*) cumulonimbus clouds, it ___________ (*rain*) in the next 24 hours.

**3** If heavy rain ___________ (*fall*) for many days, the ground ___________ (*not/be*) able to absorb any more water.

**4** If it ___________ (*snow*) heavily tonight, we ___________ (*not/go*) to school tomorrow.

**5** If you ___________ (*use*) your imagination, you ___________ (*see*) many strange shapes in the clouds.



**7** **What will happen? Read, think, and write.**

they / melt     ~~it / do / a lot of damage~~     the fog / disappear     the grass / turn yellow

**1** If hail ___________ (*fall*), ___it will do a lot of damage___.

**2** If ice crystals ___________ (*fall*) through a thin layer of warm air, ___________________________.

**3** If the weather ___________ (*be*) too dry, ___________________________.

**4** If the sun ___________ (*come*) out, ___________________________.

**8** **Read the questions. Answer for you.**

**1** Do you like the rain or does it make you feel sad? What do/don't you like about it?

___________________________________________

**2** If you wake up tomorrow and it's snowing, what will/won't you do?

___________________________________________

**3** Have you ever been in a thunderstorm? What was it like?

___________________________________________

# Earth's Surface

## What kind of processes change Earth's surface?

**1** **Unscramble the letters and write the words.**

1 ___renewable___ energy

2 _______________ energy

3 _______________ energy

4 Earth's _______________

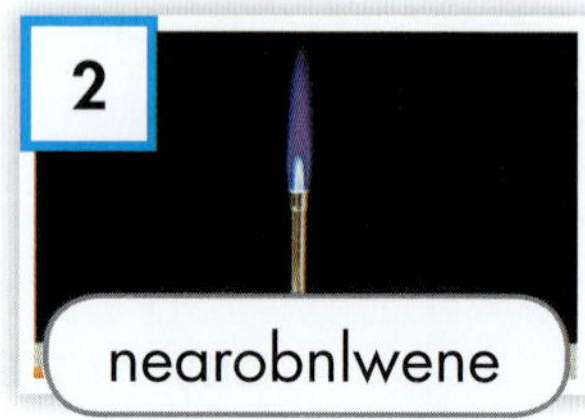

**2** **Where do we get our energy from? Match and write.**

1 Natural resources are things that _c_

2 Inexhaustible energy __

3 Nonrenewable energy __

4 Renewable energy __

**a** cannot be replaced, or, if it is replaced, it cannot be replaced fast enough.

**b** can be replaced, but only over long periods of time.

**c** exist in nature and can be used by people to produce energy.

**d** constantly and immediately replaces itself—it never runs out.

**3** **Read and write. Use words from 2.**

1 ___Inexhaustible___ energy comes from natural resources.

2 Irreplaceable energy comes from _______________ resources

3 _______________ energy comes from replaceable resources.

4 Gas, wood, and water are _______________ resources.

**4** **Where do you think the sun gets its energy?**
**Think of your own ideas. Then read and compare.**



The energy we consume every day comes from many different natural resources. It can be renewable energy, like the energy we get from burning wood to heat our homes, or it can be nonrenewable energy, like the energy we get from fossil fuels to run our cars. Then there's the energy we get from the sun, which is the most important source of energy for our planet. But where does the sun get its energy? It gets it from the nuclear energy that is generated deep inside its core. We know that, on Earth, the production of nuclear energy comes from nonrenewable resources. Does this mean that one day the sun will run out of energy? Sadly, yes, but that won't happen for another five billion years or so.

The sun gives us direct energy in the form of light and heat that make life possible on Earth, but it is also responsible for other natural resources like the wind. It may sound strange when you first hear it, but let's see how it happens. The sun's energy warms Earth's surface. The heat creates differences in temperature and air pressure. Masses of air start moving from areas of higher air pressure into areas of lower air pressure. This movement is wind, and it's a more environmentally friendly way to produce electricity.

**5** **Look at the text in 4. Read and correct the sentences.**

**1** Wood is an inexhaustible energy source.   _______ a renewable _______

**2** The sun is powered by electrical energy.   _____________________

**3** We get energy by burning fossil fuels only.   _____________________

**4** Wind is the movement of air pressure.   _____________________

**6** **Energy in your everyday life. Write about the renewable and non-renewable energy that you use.**

In the house where I live, we use _____________________ energy.
It comes from _____________________. We use / don't use any
_____________________. I would choose _____________________ because
_____________________.

# Lesson 1 · How does Earth's surface change?

**1** **Earth's surface is constantly changing. Read and write.**

> plates    fault    sliding plate boundary    spreading plate boundary
> lithosphere    converging plate boundary

**1** The ___lithosphere___ is the solid, rocky outer-most layer of Earth.

**2** Sections of the solid, rocky outermost layer of Earth are called _____________.

**3** A _____________ occurs when two plates push into each other.

**4** A _____________ occurs when plates move apart from each other.

**5** A _____________ occurs when two plates move past each other in opposite directions.

**6** A _____________ is a crack in the land where two plates meet.

**2** **Match the pictures and the words from 1. Write.**

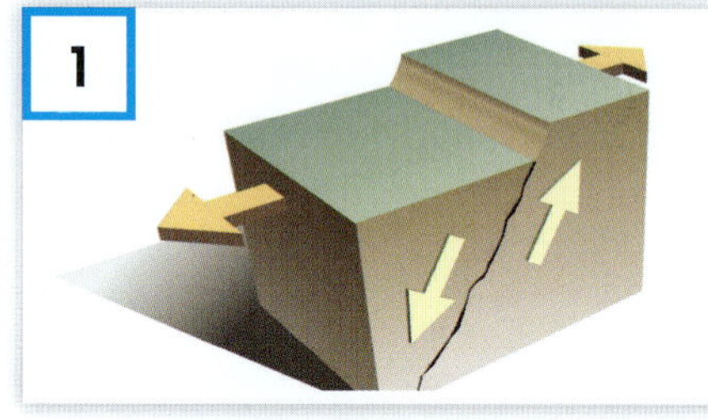

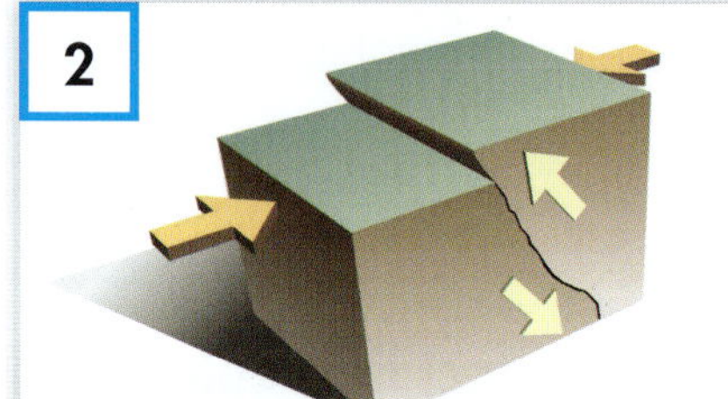

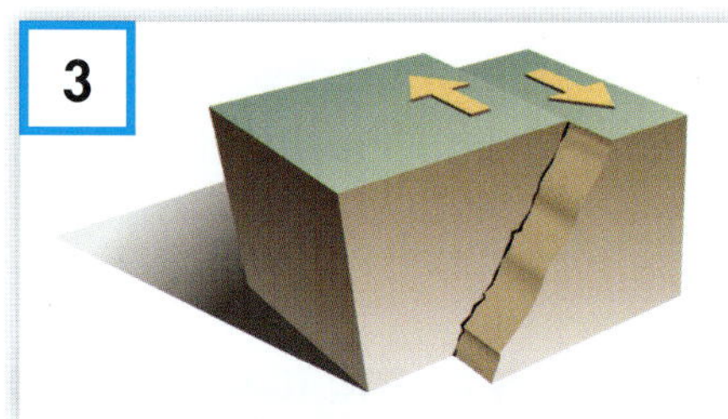

spreading plate boundary    _____________    _____________

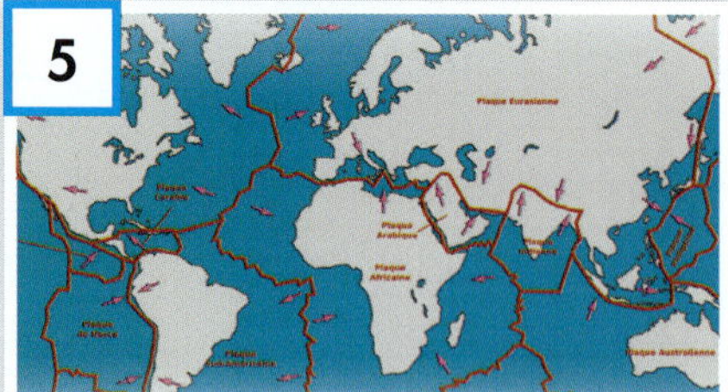

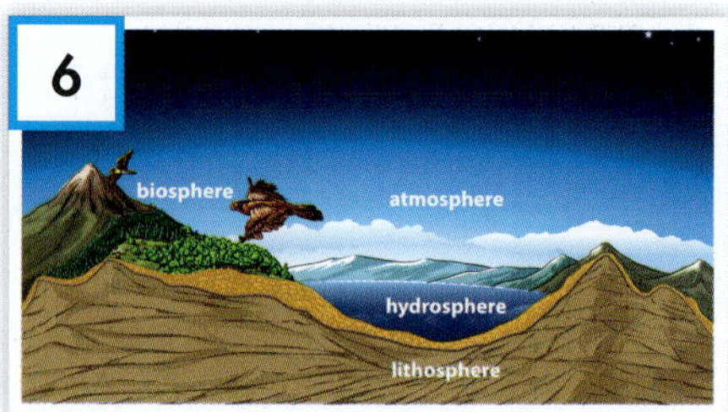


_____________    _____________    _____________

**3** **Circle the correct word.**

**1** A **constructive** / **destructive** force builds new features on Earth's surface.

**2** A **constructive** / **destructive** force wears away or tears down features on Earth's surface.

**4**  **Which globe shows Earth as it is now? What does the other globe show?**

**Reading Tip**

To get an idea of what a text is about, read it quickly without stopping to think about words you don't know or things you don't understand.

**5**  **Read and write.**

> constructive forces    plates    lithosphere    spreading
> converging    valleys    destructive forces    faults    sliding

Earth's surface is constantly changing. Some changes, like those caused by earthquakes, can be very sudden and are known as (**1**) _destructive forces_. Together with changes that happen over millions of years, they reshape the (**2**) _________________________, the outermost layer of rock that is Earth's "face". So what would our planet look like to someone who saw it from space 200 million years ago? The answer is, it would look very different.

About 270 million years ago, there was only one continent on Earth, called Pangaea, and it covered nearly one third of the planet's surface. Pangaea started to break apart about 200 million years ago. The moving pieces of the lithosphere formed Earth's continents as we know them today. It seems strange when we look at a map now, but Africa and South America were joined together until 140 million years ago. North America and Europe broke apart only 80 million years ago.

As the plates moved, they interacted with one another. As plates pushed into each other, (**3**) _____________________ plate boundaries formed, and mountains appeared. Where plates moved away from each other, (**4**) _____________________ plate boundaries formed, and valleys appeared. Where plates moved past each other in opposite directions, (**5**) _____________________ plate boundaries formed along (**6**) _____________________.

Earth's (**7**) _____________________ are moving all the time. At the moment, Africa is colliding with Europe, and the Australian plate is now colliding with Southeast Asia. In about 250 million years, Africa, North America, and South America will join Eurasia and a new Pangaea will be formed.

## Lesson 2 • What are some energy resources?

**1** Energy comes from many sources. Unscramble the letters and write the words.

**1** __biomass__ fuel

**2** _____________ energy

**3** _____________ energy

**4** _____________ energy

**2** What type of resources do these types of energy come from? Write *nonrenewable*, *inexhaustible*, or *renewable*.

**1** _____________

**resources**

geothermal, solar, wind, moving water

**2** _____________

**resources**

biomass fuels (wood, corn, etc.)

**3** _____________

**resources**

nuclear, coal, oil

**3** Facts about energy. Read and circle.

**1** We can't make biomass fuels out of _____________.

  **a** corn     **b** garbage     **c** (rock)

**2** Some biomass can be turned into _____________ that can run cars.

  **a** fuels     **b** electricity     **c** steam

**3** Burning biomass produces _____________.

  **a** garbage     **b** oxygen     **c** carbon dioxide

**4** Geothermal energy comes from the high temperatures _____________.

  **a** of the sun     **b** deep inside Earth     **c** on Earth's surface

**5** Nuclear energy generates _____________ to produce electricity.

  **a** coal     **b** steam     **c** wind

**4**  **What are the advantages and disadvantages of these types of energy? Read and write.**

**a**  It causes air pollution.

**b**  Less garbage is dumped in landfills.

**c**  It's inexhaustible.

**d**  It can be produced at home.

**e**  You need to cover very large surfaces with cells, to capture energy.

**f**  It's "green" (= environmentally friendly).

**g**  It may let out poisonous gases that are found deep inside Earth.

**h**  It works well only in areas that have a lot of sunshine all year round.

**i**  It can be produced only in areas where there are high temperatures deep inside the ground.

**j**  It's renewable.

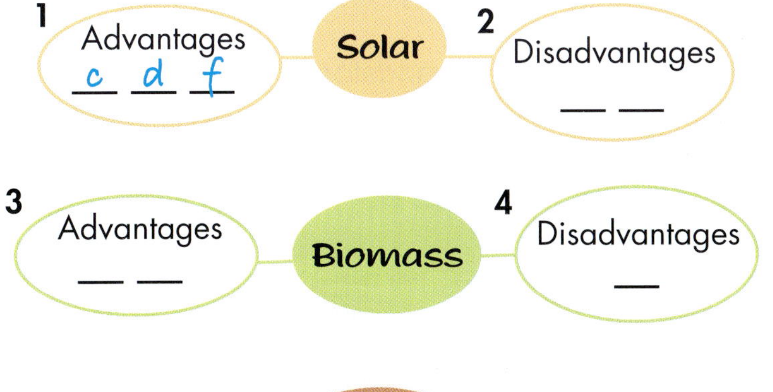




**5**  **Consequences. Read and match.**

**1**  Fossil fuels are a nonrenewable resource,

**2**  Solar panels can produce all the electricity a home needs,

**3**  New trees replace the ones we cut down,

**4**  Burning wood releases carbon dioxide into the atmosphere,

**a**  so people don't have to buy electricity from anywhere else.

**b**  so they are a renewable resource.

**c**  so, one day, they might run out.

**d**  so this way of producing energy pollutes the environment.

**1**   **Pollutants harm the planet. Match and write. Complete the sentence.**

| automobile | sandstorm | litter | forest fire | ~~landfill~~ | chemicals |

1 _landfill_    2 __________    3 __________    4 __________    5 __________    6 __________ in the water

The pictures all show examples of ____________.

**2**   **Which pollutants are the result of human actions and which are natural pollutants? Write the words from 1.**

**1**   Result of human actions: _landfill_, ____________, ____________, ____________

**2**   Natural pollutants: ____________, ____________

**3**   **What effect do these pollutants have on the environment? Match and write. Some pollutants have the same effect.**

**1**   Automobiles _c_

**2**   Sandstorms ___

**3**   Coal-burning power plants ___

**4**   Factories that dump chemicals into water ___

**5**   Volcanic eruptions ___

**6**   Leaks from tankers carrying oil ___

**7**   Forest fires ___

**8**   Litter ___

**a**   They poison and kill plants, fish, and animals that live in or near the water.

**b**   They throw dust, ash, and other particles into the air. They can block the sunlight for a long period of time. This can create winter conditions and upsets the life cycle of plants and animals.

**c**   They release harmful chemicals into the air. Plants, animals, and people are poisoned.

**d**   It spreads harmful bacteria and disease. It can harm land and sea animals.

**e**   Dust and sand covers the ground, and plants die.

**4** **Reducing pollution. Read and write.**

chemicals     forest fires     landfills     litter     sandstorm
coal-burning power plants          automobiles          ~~pollutants~~

### Be Aware – Be Informed!

Don't throw away (**1**) _pollutants_ with household garbage. Used batteries contain harmful (**2**) _____________ that are used to produce electricity. They leak into the soil in (**3**) _____________. Rain and underground water can carry them away and poison plants and animals.

Stop polluting our air! YES to solar power! NO to (**4**) _____________!

Electric (**5**) _____________: Drive into a better future. Visit our showroom for more information.

Please pick up your (**6**) _____________. Take empty bottles and food containers home with you.

### Grammar Tip

Sources of pollutants **may** be natural.

Without this sunlight, temperatures **may** drop, and plants **might** die.

How **might** acid rain harm the environment?

**5** **Rewrite the sentences using *may/might*.**

**1**   The volcanic ash will probably pollute the environment.
_The volcanic ash may/might pollute the environment._

**2**   Perhaps the chemicals I'm using will harm other organisms.

_____________________________________________

**3**   It is possible that some pollutants will harm the planet.

_____________________________________________

**4**   Without enough sunlight, the plants will probably die.

_____________________________________________

**6**   **What will the future be like if we don't protect the environment? Think of at least two ideas of your own. Write sentences using *may/might*.**

_____________________________________________

_____________________________________________

# Unit 6 — Earth and Space

**THE BIG Q — How do objects move in space?**

**1** What different objects can we find in space? Match and write.

> comet    meteors    glowing    moon    asteroid    orbit    ~~gas~~

**1** a burning _____gas_____

**2** the sun—a ball of _____________ gases

**3** planets in _____________ around the sun

**4** a _____________

**5** _____________

**6** a _____________

**7** an _____________

**2** What is it? Read the definitions, find the words in **1**, and write.

**a** _____comet_____ A frozen mass of different types of ice and dust orbiting the sun.

**b** _____________ A substance like air that has no fixed shape.

**c** _____________ When an object is shining with a warm, steady light.

**d** _____________ A natural object that revolves around a planet.

**e** _____________ A rocky object that revolves around the sun but is too small to be called a planet.

**f** _____________ An object that is moving fast through Earth's atmosphere and looks like a bright line of light.

**g** _____________ The curved path followed by natural objects that revolve around another body.

**3** How do objects move in space? Think and write. Then read the first paragraph of the text in **4**. Were your ideas correct? _______________________________

_______________________________________________________________________

**4** Read and match. Write *a* or *b*.



**a** I read somewhere that the sun is dying. What will happen to Earth?

**b** Why do objects in space orbit around other objects?

**We can answer your science questions**

**1 Q:** _______________

(Angelica, 11)

**A:** If left alone, any object in space will travel in a straight line. Or at least it will until a force makes it stop or change the way it moves. That force can be gravity. If an object passes near a large planet, it gets "caught" in the field of gravity, and it is pulled toward the center of the planet. If the force of gravity and the object's forward motion are equal, the object can't pull away from the planet, but it can't crash into it, either. The only thing it can do is go into orbit.

**2 Q:** _______________

(Nikki, 11)

**A:** Relax, the sun will be around for the next five to seven billion years. But, yes, it is using up its energy and is slowly dying. When the sun dies, Earth will disappear into the hot mass of the sun. I'm sure, however, that humans have plenty of time to think of a way to continue living, maybe on a new planet.

**5** Read the text in **4** again. Circle the correct words.

**1** If no force acts on them, objects **travel in a straight line** / **move around another object** in space.

**2** By using its energy, the sun is **killing Earth** / **dying**.

**3** When the sun dies, Earth will **freeze** / **burn**.

**6** Write about two space objects you find interesting. Explain why.

_______________________________________________________________________

_______________________________________________________________________

**1**  **What is a star? Look at the photos and write the missing letters.**

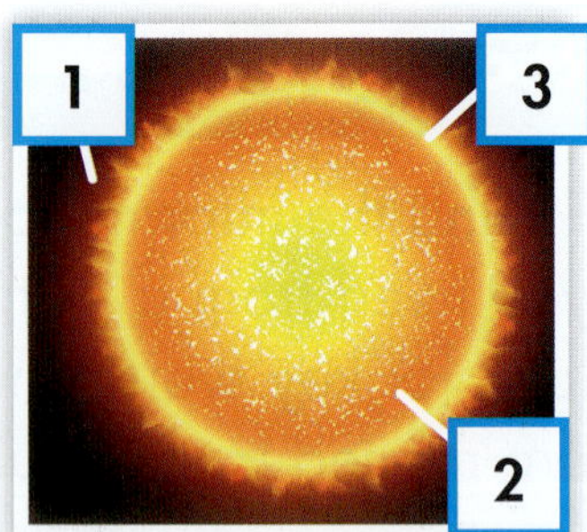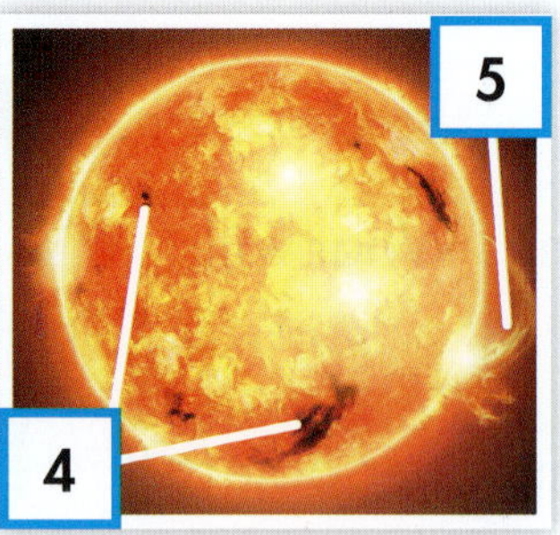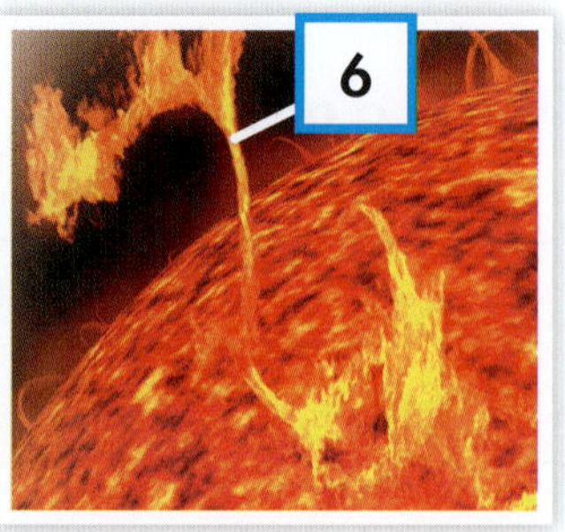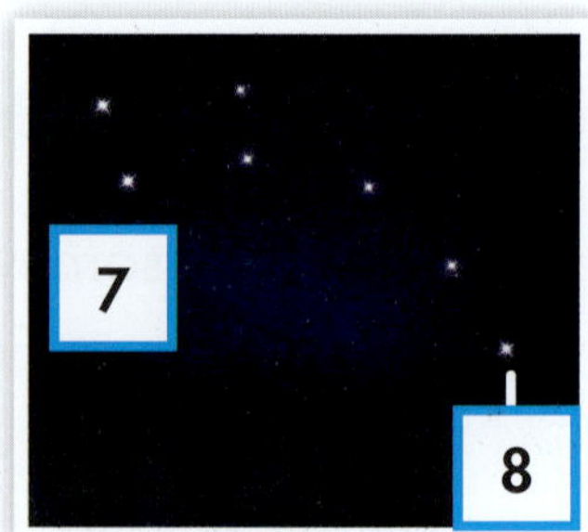

**1**  c _o_ _r_ o n _a_

**2**  p __ __ t __ s __ __ e __ e

**3**  c __ r __ m __ s __ __ r __

**4**  __ u __ s p __ __ s

**5**  p __ __ m __ n __ __ __ e

**6**  s __ __ a __ f __ __ r __ s

**7**  c __ __ s __ __ l l __ t __ __ n

**8**  P __ l __ __ i s

**2**  **Facts about the sun. Read and write words from 1.**

# Space Files

| | |
|---|---|
| **Name:** | the sun |
| **Where:** | at the heart of the solar system |
| **Size:** | medium-sized—it has 99.8% of the mass in the solar system |
| **Temperature:** | core—15 million degrees Celsius<br>surface—5,500 degrees Celsius |

**Features:**

(1) __photosphere__ —innermost layer that gives off the light we see

(2) ________________—layer between the photosphere and the corona

(3) ________________—outermost layer

(4) ________________—ribbons of glowing gases that leap out of the chromosphere and into the corona solar

(5) ________________—eruption of waves and particles into space

(6) ________________—cooler dark areas on the sun's surface

**3** **Facts about Polaris. Read and write.**

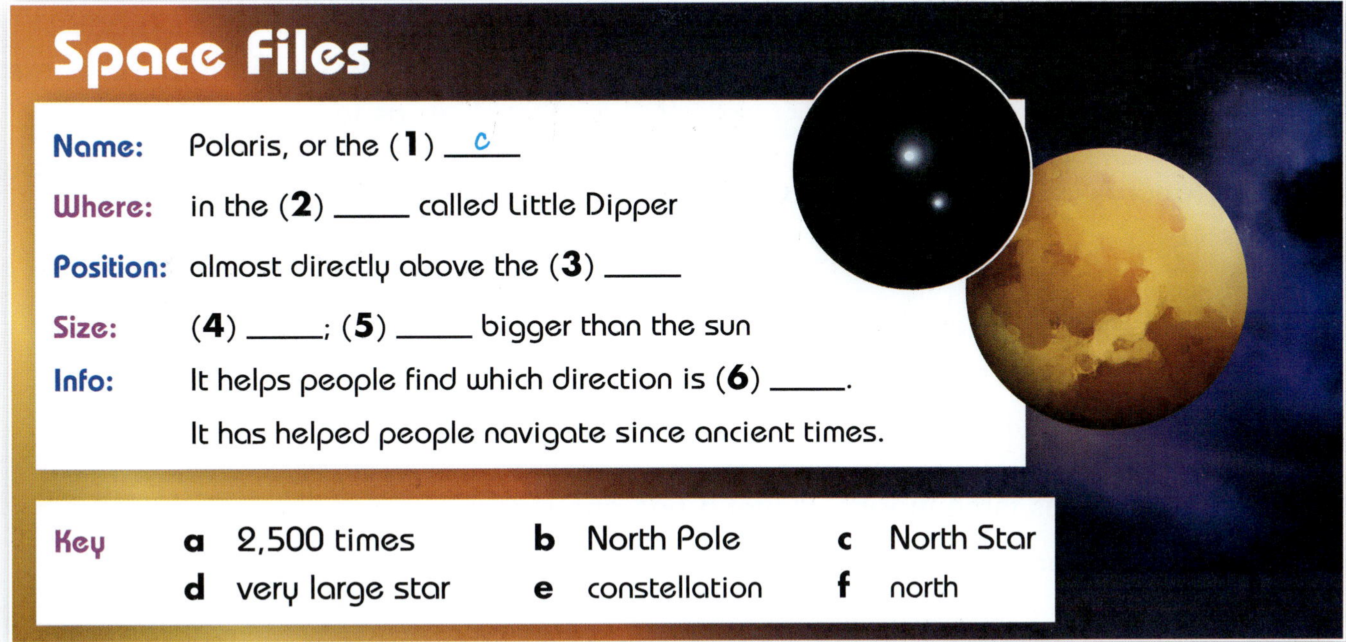



**4** **Look at 3. Circle the correct answer.**

**1** A constellation is a group of _____.

   **a** stars that we can't see   **b** moons that orbit a planet   **c** stars that form a pattern

**2** Polaris _____.

   **a** is a small star   **b** is much bigger than the sun   **c** couldn't be seen in the past

**3** The _____ is not a constellation.

   **a** Little Dipper   **b** Big Dipper   **c** North Star

**4** Polaris is special because it _____.

   **a** shows us where south is   **b** rotates around the North Pole   **c** can direct us

**5** As Earth spins the constellations _____.

   **a** seem to move, although they don't   **b** move with it   **c** move in the opposite direction

**5** **Which constellations do you know? Write names.**

_____________________________________________

**6** **Read and write about two planets. Use *as…as* and the words in the box.**

| hot | ~~big~~ | small | long | many moons |

**1** Planet A is smaller than planet B.

Planet A isn't ___*as big as*___ planet B.

**2** The temperature of planet A is twice the temperature of planet B.

Planet A is twice _____________ planet B.

**3** Planet A has three moons. Planet B has one moon.

Planet B doesn't have _____________ planet A.

**4** A day is 20 hours long on planet A. It is 21 hours long on planet B.

A day on planet A is almost _____________ a day on planet B.

**5** Planet A's moons are big. Planet B's moon is small.

Planet A's moons aren't _____________ Planet B's moon.



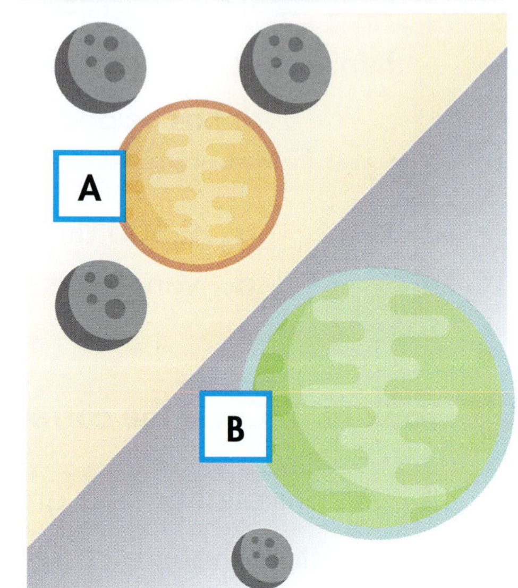

**7** **Read and write about a new planet, Kepler-452b. Use (*not*) as…as.**

# KEPLER-452B

On July 23, 2015, NASA announced the discovery of a planet that is so similar to Earth that it could probably be Earth's "cousin". Its name is Kepler-452b.

Kepler-452b is 1.6 times **(1)** ___*as big as Earth*___ (**big** / **Earth**). The planet's gravity is twice Earth's gravity. On Kepler-452b, an object is twice **(2)** _____________ (**heavy** / **it is on Earth**).

The planet probably has an atmosphere, but the atmosphere on Earth is **(3)** _____________ (**not** / **thick** / **the atmosphere on Kepler-452b**).

The sunlight is **(4)** _____________ (**bright** / **our sunlight**).

It gets about **(5)** _____________ (**much energy from its sun** / **Earth**).

A year is almost **(6)** _____________ (**long** / **an Earth year**).

The planet takes 385 days to orbit its star, very similar to Earth's 365-day year.

**1** **There are lots of different objects in space. Match and write.**

> asteroid    ~~moons~~    comet    dwarf planet

**1** ___moons___   **3** ___________ belt

**2** ___________   **4** ___________

**2** **Mark (✓) the correct sentences.**

**1 a** Asteroids are rocky masses.

**b** Asteroids are made of ice and dust.

**2 a** The asteroid belt is located between Earth and Mars.

**b** The asteroid belt is located between Mars and Jupiter.

**3 a** Larger asteroids orbit smaller asteroids.

**b** Smaller asteroids orbit larger asteroids.

**4 a** Asteroids revolve around the sun.

**b** Asteroids revolve around the planets.

**5 a** Earth has never been hit by an asteroid.

**b** Asteroids hit Earth in the past.

**3** **Are these sentences true for comets (C) or meteors (M)? Read and write C or M.**

**1** They're also called shooting stars.

**2** They're a frozen mass of different types of ice and dust.

**3** They pass through the solar system and orbit the sun.

**4** When they enter Earth's atmosphere, they heat up and glow.

**5** They sometimes look like a star that keeps changing its position in the sky.

**4** **Describe "the life of a meteor". Put the sentences in order 1–6.**

**a** If it doesn't burn up completely, a <u>meteor</u> hits Earth's surface.

**b** Meteors heat up and glow. As they fall, they look like a streak of light.

**c** When a <u>meteoroid</u> hits Earth's atmosphere, it becomes a meteor.

**d** Some meteoroids are pieces of rock that have broken off an <u>asteroid</u> or a comet.   *1*

**e** A piece of meteor that lands on Earth is called a <u>meteorite</u>.

**f** Most meteors burn up before they hit Earth's surface.

**5** **"The life of a meteor". Label the picture with the underlined words in 4.**

**6** **Is Pluto a planet? Read and write.**

| | | | |
|---|---|---|---|
| asteroid | solar system | meteoroid | ~~orbits~~ |
| dwarf planet | moons | comets | objects |

Posted: September 25th

It used to be thought of as the ninth planet in our solar system. But then scientists had a closer look at it, and decided that Pluto wasn't a planet. Planets must clear the region around their **(1)** _____orbits_____, and Pluto doesn't do that. Although Pluto's gravity attracts five **(2)** ___________ that orbit around it, it is not strong enough either to attract or to push away other **(3)** ___________ in Pluto's path. Pluto is too small to be a planet, but it is also too big to be an **(4)** ___________. It is quite different, too. Pluto is now classified as a **(5)** ___________. It is a new name that is given to all space objects that are like Pluto. Scientists now believe that there could be as many as 200 of them in our **(6)** ___________.

**7** **Complete the sentences. Write *so ... that* and the words in parentheses.**

**1** Jupiter's gravity is ___so strong that___ it holds most asteroids away from Earth. (strong)

**2** Meteors move through the atmosphere _______________ they heat up very quickly. (fast)

**3** Some comets are _______________ they can be seen without a telescope. (large)

**4** When they're nearer the sun, comets become _______________ they start melting. (hot)

**5** At certain times each year, there are _______________ it looks as though it's raining fire. (many meteors)

**6** The impact of a meteor on Earth can be _______________ it can form a crater up to twenty four times the size of the meteor. (forceful)

> **Grammar Tip**
>
> When a meteor shoots through the air, it gets **so hot that** it glows.
> Titan has an atmosphere **so thick that** it lets little light pass through it.

**8** **Match and write sentences. Use *so ... that.***

**1** Some meteors are small.

**2** Pluto's gravity is weak.

**3** Pluto's orbit is odd.

**4** Mercury is close to the sun.

**5** The sun is hot.

**a** Sometimes it is closer to the sun than Neptune.

**b** The sun pulls everything away from Mercury's orbit.

**c** It cannot clear the region around its orbit.

**d** They burn up completely before they fall to Earth.

**e** Anything that goes near it burns.

**1** Some meteors are so small that they burn up completely before they fall to Earth.

**2** _______________

**3** _______________

**4** _______________

**5** _______________

# Review 4–6

**1** Do the quiz. Circle *a*, *b*, or *c*.

**1** Sleet, hail, and snow are all examples of __.

  **a** rain      **b** atmosphere      **c** precipitation

**2** __ clouds are high level clouds.

  **a** Fog      **b** Stratus      **c** Cirrus

**3** The pushing force of the atmosphere is called __ pressure.

  **a** barometric      **b** humidity      **c** altitude

**4** A __ may include continents, parts of the ocean floor, or both.

  **a** boundary      **b** landfill      **c** plate

**5** __ is an inexhaustible source of energy.

  **a** Biomass      **b** Geothermal energy      **c** Natural gas

**6** __ resources never run out.

  **a** Nonrenewable      **b** Inexhaustible      **c** Renewable

**7** A __ plate boundary forms when two plates move apart from each other.

  **a** spreading      **b** converging      **c** sliding

**8** Earth and Mars are the only planets that have __.

  **a** asteroids      **b** moons      **c** sunspots

**9** A piece of a meteor that lands on Earth is called a __.

  **a** meteoroid      **b** comet      **c** meteorite

**10** The region between Mars and Jupiter is called the __ belt.

  **a** asteroid      **b** prominence      **c** meteoroid

You get one point for each correct answer. What's your score?

**1–3** Oh dear!    **4–5** OK.    **6–8** Very good!    **9–10** Excellent!

**2** **What are the words? Read the clues and write the words. Then find the words in the word search puzzle. They can be in these directions:** → ↗ ↘ ↓

| | | | | | | | | | | | | | | | |
|---|---|---|---|---|---|---|---|---|---|---|---|---|---|---|---|
| H | T | O | S | L | I | D | I | N | G | K | C | Q | T | H | N |
| M | G | Y | O | Z | F | G | S | S | Z | Z | R | H | O | U | P |
| Z | T | H | D | J | E | G | C | T | K | K | A | C | S | W | Z |
| A | T | R | E | W | P | H | B | P | P | V | T | F | U | S | G |
| Y | F | T | A | G | A | O | F | N | P | U | E | L | A | L | J |
| Z | Q | D | W | D | J | R | L | U | C | Z | R | A | N | P | E |
| L | A | Y | C | Z | E | K | F | L | O | K | K | O | N | Y | T |
| D | L | V | O | E | X | W | J | P | U | H | I | W | J | P | S |
| Y | T | G | G | O | I | K | I | K | L | T | D | A | O | N | T |
| M | I | Z | B | J | H | O | C | N | A | A | A | N | G | R | R |
| Q | T | N | Y | E | C | G | E | L | D | C | N | N | U | W | E |
| W | U | K | M | G | O | E | L | F | D | S | D | E | T | Q | A |
| C | D | M | Y | W | L | E | I | X | B | B | D | X | T | O | M |
| Y | E | C | L | I | T | H | O | S | P | H | E | R | E | T | Z |

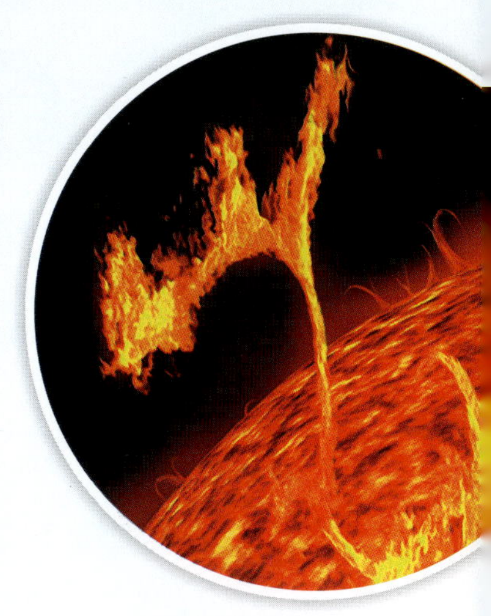

**1** This tells you how high above the ocean a place is. (8 letters) *altitude*

**2** This is a narrow band of high-speed wind that can affect local weather. (2 words: 3 and 6 letters)

**3** These are winds that blow almost constantly near the equator. (2 words: 5 and 5 letters)

**4** This is the solid, rocky outermost layer of Earth (11 letters)

**5** This is an unwanted substance added to the water, air, or soil. (9 letters)

**6** This describes plate boundaries that move past each other in opposite directions. (7 letters)

**7** This can form on the surface of Earth when it is hit by a meteor. (6 letters)

**8** This is a star, a hot ball of glowing gases. (3 letters)

**9** This is a large, round object that revolves around the sun, but has not cleared the region around its orbit. (2 words: 5 and 6 letters)

# Matter

## What are the properties of matter?

**1** The properties of matter can change. Look at the pictures. Read and write.

> chemical change    physical change    solution
> water vapor    mixture    evaporate    freezes

**1** When it's very cold, the surface of a lake ___*freezes*___.

**2** When water boils, it ___________. ___________ rises into the air.

**3** Lemonade is a ___________ of water, sugar, and lemon juice.

**4** The bowl contains a ___________ of nuts.

**5** When iron rusts, it goes through a ___________.

**6** When a newspaper is rolled up, it goes through a ___________.

**2** Examples of physical and chemical changes in everyday life. Read and write the answers in your notebook.

**1** After you've washed your hair, it's wet. How does it become dry again?

**2** What happens to lemonade if you put it in the freezer for a few hours?

**3** Are the changes in 1 and 2 physical or chemical?

**4** What are some examples of mixtures and solutions from your everyday life?

**5** We use milk to make yogurt. Is it a physical or a chemical change? Why?

**3** **What is everything made of? Read and write. There are two extra words.**

| | | |
|---|---|---|
| properties | water vapor | solution |
| chemical | evaporates | mixture |
| freezes | physical | ~~matter~~ |



## The Physical and Chemical Properties of Materials

What do you, I, and every single thing you can see or feel around you have in common? We are all made of tiny moving particles of **(1)** _____matter_____. So, if everything is made of the same thing, how can we tell things apart? Well, there are different forms of matter, with different **(2)** _____________. Physical characteristics also make us different. You and I are made of the same matter, but we are not the same height or weight, eye or skin color. Different forms of matter are found all over the universe, but, on Earth, we find matter in three main forms: solids, liquids, and gases. Water is a liquid. When water **(3)** _____________, it becomes ice. When it boils, it **(4)** _____________—it turns into water vapor. Ice and water vapor are different from water because ice is a solid and water vapor is a gas. These physical properties of matter are the kind of qualities or characteristics that we can observe without changing what material it is. When an object changes any of these properties, it goes through a **(5)** _____________ change.

We can also tell things apart by their chemical properties. We can only see the changes in those properties if there is a chemical reaction with another material. When a **(6)** _____________ change happens, it can't change back! For example, when paper burns, it can't change back into unburned paper. Physical changes are not like that. If **(7)** _____________ cools down, it becomes liquid water again.

**4** **Look at the text in 3. Circle _T_ (true) or _F_ (false).**

**1** Everything is made from the same type of matter.     T /(F)

**2** We can tell things apart by their characteristics.     T / F

**3** There are at least three forms of matter on Earth.     T / F

**4** We can see the chemical properties of matter.     T / F

# Lesson 1 · What are solids, liquids, and gases?

**1** **The state of matter can change. Match and write.**

> melting/freezing point    boiling point    volume
> condensation    plasma    evaporation

volume

**2** **Read and circle the correct words.**

**1** Matter can change its **state** / **point** at certain temperatures.

**2** Gases do not have a definite **volume** / **state**, so they can be squeezed to fit a small container.

**3** **Electricity** / **Plasma** is a state of matter.

**4** After the **condensation** / **evaporation** of salt water, the white dust that is left behind is salt.

**5** The **freezing** / **boiling** point of a liquid is the same as the melting point of its solid state.

**6** When water vapor touches a very cold surface, **condensation** / **freezing** forms.

**3** What happens when matter changes its state? Complete the chart.

| Change | State |
| --- | --- |
| **(1)** _melting_ point | from solid to liquid |
| freezing point | **(2)** ______________ |
| **(3)** ______________ | from liquid to gas |
| boiling point | **(4)** ______________ |
| **(5)** ______________ | from gas to liquid |



The particles **of a gas** are far apart. If the temperature **of a liquid** is high enough, particles will change to a gas.

**4** How do particles behave? Read and write.

> liquid     solid     gas     container     metal     material

**1** If placed in a container, the particles of a ______ gas ______ will spread out evenly.

**2** One of the properties of a ______________ is that it can conduct electricity.

**3** The particles of a ______________ slow down as it gets colder.

**4** The melting point of a ______________ can identify it.

**5** A liquid has a definite volume, but takes the shape of its ______________.

**6** The particles of a ______________ move by vibrating in place.

Plasma ball

**5** Think about your everyday life. Write examples.

**1** Condensation: _Water droplets that form on the outside surface of a glass of cold water on a hot day._

**2** Evaporation: ______________________________________________

**3** Melting point (of a material): ______________________________

**4** Freezing point (of a material): ______________________________

**5** Boiling point (of a material): ______________________________

## Lesson 2 · What are mixtures and solutions?

**1** **Read and write the missing letters.**

**1** A m _i_ _x_ _t_ u _r_ e of different fruits.

**2** The pasta is s __ p __ __ a __ ed from the water it boiled in.

**3** The s __ l __ bi __ i __ y of sun tea increases at high temperatures.

**4** This is a s __ l __ __ i __ n of chocolate and milk.

**5** This is the s __ __ u __ e .

**6** This is the __ ol __ en __ .

**2** **Correct the sentences. Change one or two words.**

**1** In a ~~solution~~, each material keeps its own properties. ___*mixture*___

**2** Different parts of a mixture cannot be separated from the rest of the mixture. ___________

**3** In a solution, solutes spread out evenly and will immediately settle or separate. ___________

**4** Water is not a good solvent. It can't dissolve many substances. ___________

**5** You can make solids dissolve more quickly in a solution by leaving or cooling it. ___________

**6** Different substances have the same solubility in water. ___________

**3** **What mixtures and solutions do you use in your daily life? Think and write sentences.**

| Mixture | Solution |
| --- | --- |
| I eat salad with my lunch and dinner. It is a mixture of vegetables. | I drink hot chocolate for breakfast. It is a solution of chocolate and milk. |
| ___________ | ___________ |

**4** **How do we use mixtures and solutions in everyday life? Read and write. Use the words in parentheses.**



**1** You added salt to the soup in your bowl, and now it is too salty. There's more soup left in the pot. What could you do to make your soup less salty? (*solution, solvent, solute*)

The soup and salt in my bowl are _a solution_.
To make it less salty, I could
_add more solvent to the solution_, so I will add more ______________. This way there will be less ______________ in the ______________.

**2** You want to make chocolate milk. You put a few pieces of chocolate into cold milk, but they haven't dissolved. What could you do to make them dissolve? (*solubility, material, temperature*)

I know that ________________________________________________

**3** You bought a bag of mixed nuts to have as a snack, but it has raisins in it. You don't like raisins. What could you do? (*mixture, separate*)

The nuts and raisins are a ________________________________________

**5** **What could you do in these situations? Make suggestions. Write sentences with *could*.**

**1** "I'd like to separate iron filings from sand."
use / magnet _You could use a magnet_.

**2** "I don't like blueberries in my fruit salad."
separate / mixture ______________________________

**3** "There isn't enough sugar in my lemonade."
add / your glass ______________________________

**4** "How can I make hot cocoa?"
dissolve / cocoa / in hot milk ______________________________

**5** "My tea is too hot to drink."
add / ice cubes ______________________________

**6** "I can't dissolve more sugar in this amount of liquid."
heat / solution ______________________________

**1** **Match the words to the meanings. Write the words.**

> chemical change     physical change     temperature
> melting point     substance

**1** _melting point_  The temperature at which a solid turns into liquid.

**2** _______________  A particular type of liquid, solid, or gas.

**3** _______________  When one or more types of matter change into other types of matter with different properties.

**4** _______________  When some properties of matter change but the type of matter doesn't change.

**5** _______________  A measure of how hot or cold a place or thing is.

**2** **What type of change is it? Write C (chemical change) or P (physical change).**

**3** **Look at the science website in 4. Read and circle the best title.**

**a** Chemical Changes in Everyday life.

**b** Knowing When Chemical Changes Happen.

**c** The Difference Between Physical Changes and Chemical Changes.

**4** **Choose the best title for each paragraph. There is one extra title.**

**a** Chemical Changes and the Human Body
**b** Chemical Changes and Food

**c** Food Safety
**d** Types of Changes

**1** _______________________

Physical and chemical changes happen all the time. Physical changes are easy to see because we experience them with our senses—we can see and hear glass break, and we peel fruit with our hands. Chemical changes are harder to detect. They happen when the atoms in matter rearrange themselves to form a new type of matter with different properties.

**2** _______________________

A number of chemical changes take place inside the human body in order to produce energy. One of the most important chemical changes is how our body uses food for energy. The human body uses chemicals in our digestive system to break down the food we eat. These chemical changes produce fuel for the cells and keep our bodies alive and healthy.

**3** _______________________

Much of the food we eat is a product of chemical change. We drink milk in the form that we find it, but, to make cheese or yogurt from milk, there has to be a chemical change that will turn it into a different substance. Some of the changes in food happen naturally, like the ripening of fruit. Other changes are the result of human understanding of how different substances can react to produce different chemical changes, for example, the changes that occur during baking. In fact, most ways of cooking are nothing but the creation of chemical changes that will make some food easier, more pleasant, or safer to eat.

**5** **Think about four foods that you eat. In your notebook, write answers to the questions.**

**1** Do they involve substances that go through a chemical change? Do they involve high temperatures? What are the original substances?

**2** Do they involve substances that go through only a physical change?

Unit 8

# Forces and Motion

## THE BIG ? What affects the motion of objects?

**1 Objects in motion. Unscramble the letters and write the words.**

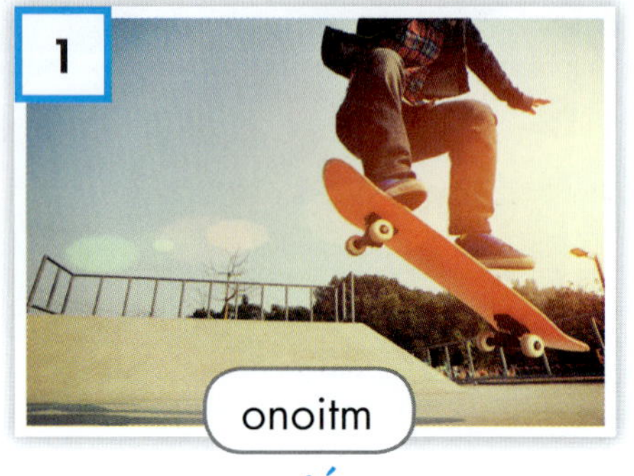

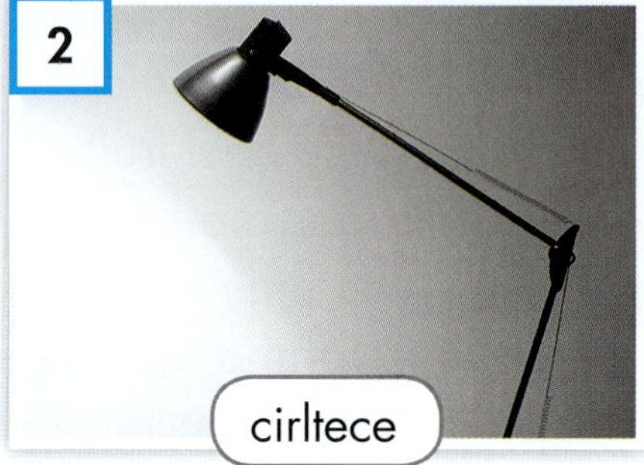

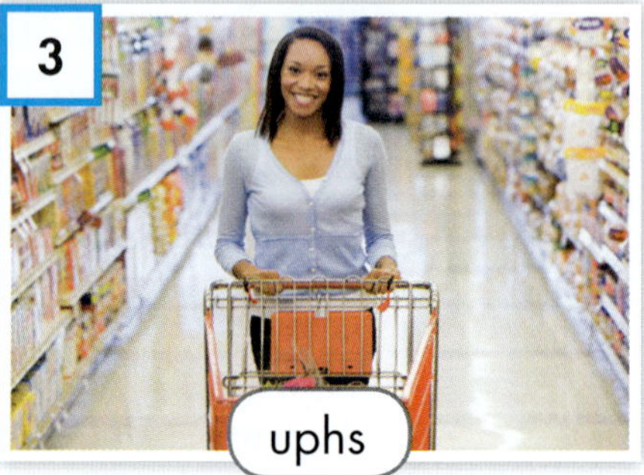

1 

onoitm

motion

2 

cirltece

______

3 

uphs

______

4 

ulpl

______

5 

amceintg

______

6 

rtiygva

______

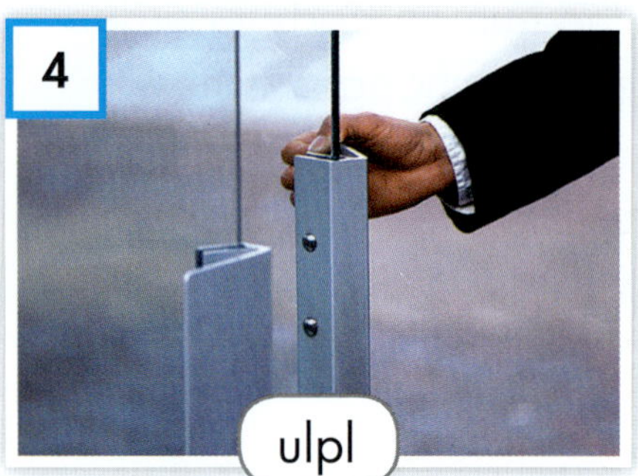

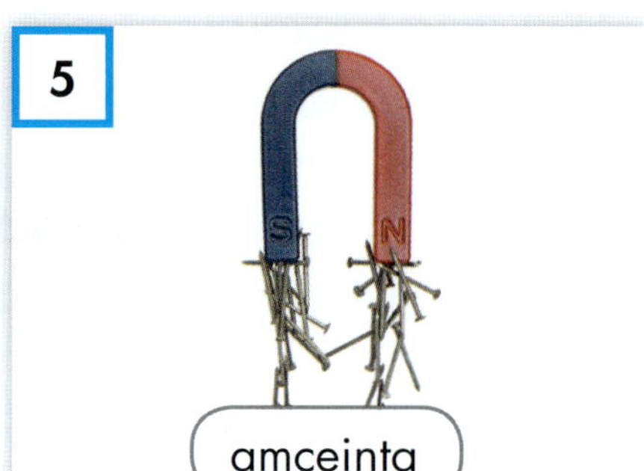

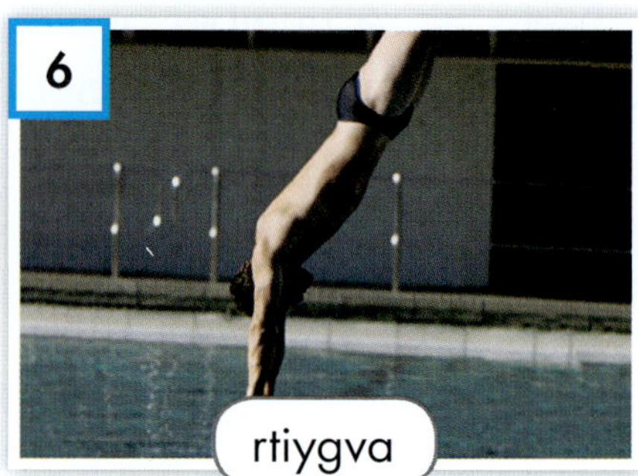

**2 Forces. Answer the questions. Write the words from 1.**

**1** Which force keeps fridge magnets stuck on the fridge door? magnetic

**2** Which force keeps you from flying up in the sky? ______

**3** Which force makes your computer work? ______

**4** Which force helps you move a shopping cart? ______

**5** Which force helps you open a car door to get in? ______

**6** What kind of forces are the forces in 1–5? They are forces that cause ______.

**3** Which force would it be impossible for life on Earth to exist without? Write one word. Quickly read the text in **4**, and check. ________________________________________

**4** Complete the text with the missing phrases. Write letters a–e.

> **Q: What would the world be like without gravity?**
>
> Without the force of gravity, the world would be nothing like we know it. The good thing is that gravity depends on mass. **(1)** _d_, its gravity can't change.
>
> Imagine that Earth's gravity was "turned off." We call this state "zero" gravity. **(2)** ___, objects would have no reason to stay down. Everything that is not fixed in place would start to float in the air. **(3)** ___, one way to overcome this problem would be to attach magnets to everything. People could wear magnetic "shoes" and walk on tracks that could use electric force to turn them into magnets. It would make motion very difficult, **(4)** ___.
>
> Water stays on our planet because of gravity. Without gravity, liquids would not stay on the planet's surface—there would be no oceans, lakes, or rivers on Earth. They would evaporate into space. Earth's atmosphere would do the same. We cannot live without water or air, **(5)** ___.

**a** Since magnetic force is a completely different force from gravity

**b** but not impossible

**c** so we would have to look for another planet with these two things

**d** As long as Earth's mass stays the same

**e** Because there would be no pull toward the center of the planet



Make sure you follow the logical connection between sentences. Look out for words like *so, because, but, since, as long as, though,* etc.

**5** Look at the text in **4**. Circle *T* (true) or *F* (false).

**1** Earth's gravity would change if Earth's mass changed.    (T)/ F

**2** Everything that is fixed to the ground would float in zero gravity.    T / F

**3** Without gravity, there is no magnetic force.    T / F

**4** Electric force can be used to create magnetic force.    T / F

**5** Earth's atmosphere stays in place because of gravity.    T / F

## Lesson 1 · What are forces?

**1** What forces are acting in these situations? Write the missing letters.

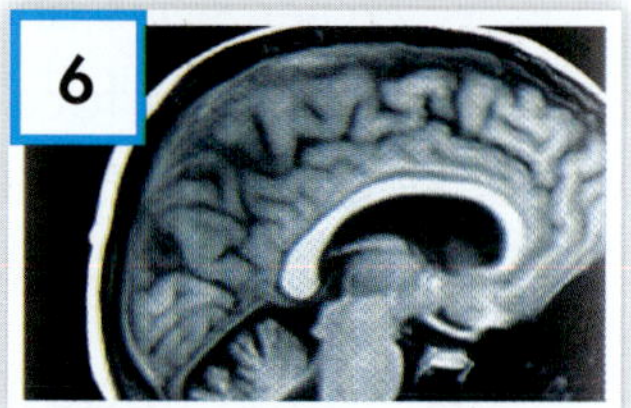

**1** b _a_ l _a_ _n_ c _e_ d _f_ _o_ rc _e_ s

**2** __ r __ c t __ __ n

**3** __ i __ r __ s __ __ __ a n __ e

**4** g __ a __ __ t __

**5** e __ __ c __ r __ c  force

**6** MRI machines use __ l e __ __ r __ m __ g __ __ t s.

**2** Match the words to the meanings. Write the words from **1**.

**a** _electric force_ The force that acts between objects that are electrically charged.

**b** ______________ When particles of air come into contact with a moving surface and resist its movement.

**c** ______________ The force that results when the contact between two materials prevents sliding.

**d** ______________ The force that pulls all objects toward the center of Earth.

**e** ______________ Two forces with the same magnitude that act in opposite directions.

**f** ______________ They can have the direction of their north and south poles switched.

**3** Circle the correct words.

**1** **Contact** / **Noncontact** forces act at a distance.

**2** **Contact** / **Noncontact** forces act when two objects touch at some point.

**4** **Which forces apply when a ball is thrown in the air? Complete the sentences using the words from the box. You can use each word more than once.**

> downward    gravity    push
> upward    stronger    weaker    move

**1** The ball is thrown up in the air: In the beginning, the ____*push*____ is ____________ than ____________, so the ball moves ____________.

**2** The ball stops moving in midair: At some point, ____________ and ____________ become equal forces, so the ball doesn't ____________.

**3** The ball starts falling toward the ground: Now, ____________ is ____________ than the ____________, and the ball is pulled ____________ toward Earth.

**5** **What role does forces play in sports? Read and write.**

> pulls    air resistance    balanced force    increase    motion    gravity
> pushes    friction    increase    reduce    contact force

All sports make use of different forces to produce a result. In basketball, a (**1**) ____*contact force*____ is applied to the ball to make it move—the player (**2**) ____________ the ball to the ground. The ball hits the ground, and the force of the contact with it makes the ball move in the opposite direction. When the player throws the ball toward the basket, the force of the push overcomes (**3**) ____________ before the ball starts falling. The ball doesn't fall to the ground immediately because there are two forces acting on it at the same time: gravity (**4**) ____________ it toward the ground, and the push makes it continue its forward motion. These two combined forces make the ball travel in a curve and fall through the basket. (**5**) ____________ is as important as gravity in a basketball game because, without it, the players' feet would slip on the smooth floor.

(**6**) ____________ is a type of friction that affects sky divers. Sky divers use parachutes that (**7**) ____________ the magnitude of the force to help them fall more slowly.

**6  Facts about forces. Read and match.**



**Grammar Tip**

Friction is the force that results when two materials **rub against** each other. The amount of friction between two objects **depends on** whether or not the surfaces are wet.

**1**  To make an electric light bulb work, you <u>turn</u>

**2**  If an object is already moving, a push may <u>speed</u>

**3**  The amount of friction between two objects also <u>depends</u>

**4**  To stop an electric machine working, we <u>turn</u>

**5**  If friction is applied to a moving wheel, it will <u>slow</u>

**a**  <u>up</u> its movement.

**b**  <u>on</u> a switch.

**c**  <u>off</u> a switch.

**d**  <u>on</u> the objects' textures and shapes.

**e**  <u>down</u> its movement.

**7  Read and write. Use the underlined phrasal verbs from 6. You may need to change the form of the verb.**

**1**  Electromagnets can be ___turned on___ or ______________.

**2**  Parachutes use air resistance to ______________ the fall of a skydiver.

**5**  You can ______________ the movement of an object by reducing the amount of friction.

**6**  The speed of an object ______________ the magnitude of the force that makes it move.

**8  Explain what forces apply when you play your favorite sport. Look at the text in 5 on page 67, to help you. Try to use at least one phrasal verb from 6.**

My favorite sport is ______________. When I ____________________________,

______________________________________________________________

______________________________________________________________

# Lesson 2 · What are machines?

**1** **What types of machines are these? Unscramble the letters and write the words. Then complete the description with one word.**

They are all ______________ machines.

_pulley_

______________ plane



______________

______________

______________ and axle

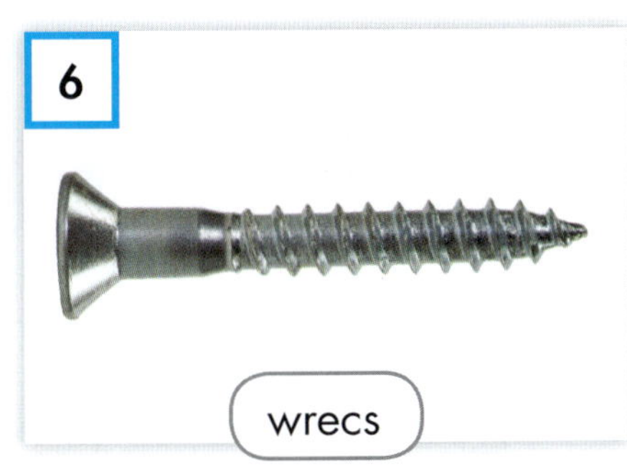


______________

**2** **Match and write. There are three extra words.**

> load    ramp    fulcrum    matter    wedge    ~~simple machine~~
> complex machine    output force    input force/effort

**1** A machine that is made up of one or two parts. _simple machine_

**2** A machine that uses two or more simple machines. ______________

**3** The amount of force you use to do work. ______________

**4** The force that a machine supplies. ______________

**5** The object that is moved with the use of a machine. ______________

**6** A fixed point or a support—the bar of a lever moves around it. ______________

**3** Look at the photo and read the sentences.
Circle *T* (true) or *F* (false).

**1** The two boys are using a complex machine.  T / **F**

**2** The type of the machine in the photo is a lever.  T / F

**3** The yellow seats at the end of the bar are the fulcrums.  T / F

**4** The boy in the blue T-shirt is the load.  T / F

**5** Both boys provide the input force.  T / F

**6** The input and output forces are at equal distances from the fulcrum.  T / F

**4** What do you use these things for? What types of simple machines are they?
Write sentences.

**1** (crack a nut) _I use a nutcracker to crack a nut. A nutcracker is a lever._

**2** (cut a piece of paper) _______________________________

**3** (open a door) _______________________________

**4** (seal a bottle) _______________________________

**5** (move a wheelchair up some steps) _______________________________

**5** Which simple machines do you use? Can you think of a complex machine that you use?
Write sentences.

_______________________________
_______________________________
_______________________________

**6** **How do machines help us? Read and write. Use *can be* and the correct form of the verb in parentheses.**



**1** The direction of a force _can be changed_ by a simple machine. (change)

**2** Doors _________________ from moving with a wedge. (stop)

**3** A lighter object _________________ more easily than a heavier object. (move)

**4** Two pieces of wood _________________ together by a screw. (pull)

**7** **Rewrite the sentences using *can be*.**

**1** You can change the direction of a force by using a lever.
The direction _of a force can be changed by using a lever._

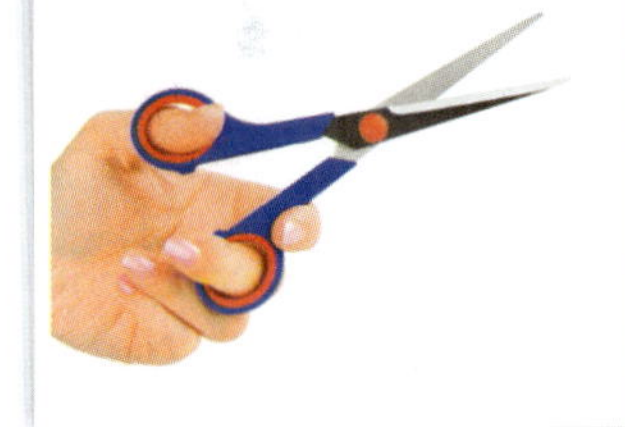

**2** You can use a crane to lift and carry heavy loads.
A crane _________________________________________.

**3** You can lift a car by using a car jack.
A car jack _________________________________________.

**4** You can fit a ramp over steps to help wheelchair users.
A ramp _________________________________________.

**8** **Draw a picture of one of the complex machines in the box. Label the different simple machines that it is made of. In your notebook, write about what it can be used for.**

scissors    a lawn mower    a crane    a bike    a skateboard

# 9 Energy

**How is energy transferred and transformed?**

**1** **What is the difference between transferring and transforming energy? Read and match.**

**1** transform energy

**a** To move energy from one place or object to another place or object.

**2** transfer energy

**b** To change one type of energy into another type of energy.

**2** **Different kinds of energy. Read and write.**

light energy     sound energy     transferred     transformed

**1** Musical instruments produce
__sound energy__.

**2** The sun provides ___________________.

**3** Electrical energy is ___________________ into light energy.

**4** The kinetic energy of the wave is ___________________ to the surfer.

**3** **Is energy transferred or transformed? Read the examples and write explanations.**

**1** A plant uses light to make food.
__The light energy from the sun is transformed into chemical energy to produce food.__

**2** A drummer hits a drum with a stick, and produces a sound.

___________________________________________

**3** A water turbine produces electricity.

___________________________________________

**4** **Read the Mad Scientist's blog. Put the sentences in the correct order. Write a–d.**

# Energy and H2O
## by The Mad Scientist

I was walking my dog, H2O, today, when I saw a friend and her son, Jack. Jack asked me an interesting question: what makes H2O walk? Do you know the answer?

You might think it's his leg muscles or his skeletal system, and you're not completely wrong. But the correct answer is the sun. This is because, in our world, nothing happens without the transformation of energy, and the source of most energy on the planet is the sun. To help you understand the connection between the sun shining and H2O walking, I have written down the connecting stages. But they're in the wrong order. See if you can put them in the right order.

**a** Finally, this chemical energy is transformed into mechanical energy by H2O's body functions. The mechanical energy of H2O's legs moving is then transformed into kinetic energy. He's walking!

**b** To begin with, matter on the surface of the sun is changed into the form of electromagnetic energy that we call light.

**c** Animals eat plants. Dogs eat the animals that eat the plants. As H2O digests his food, the chemical energy stored in the cells of the plants is transferred into H2O's cells.

**d** Some of the solar energy that is transferred from the sun to Earth is transformed into chemical energy by plants. This chemical energy is stored in the plant cells.

**1** ___________  **2** ___________

**3** ___________  **4** ___________

### Reading Tip

You need to be able to follow the sequence of events to understand how a process happens. Use your logic (i.e., which step should logically come before another) and clues in the text (i.e., words like *first, to begin with, finally, in the end*, etc.).

## Lesson 1 · What is energy?

**1** **There are different types of energy. Unscramble the letters and write the words.**

_____elastic_____ potential energy

_______________ energy

_______________ potential energy

_______________ energy

This building has been _______________

**2** **Facts about energy. Write, using phrases from 1.**

1 _____Energy_____ is the ability to do work or cause a change.

2 _______________ is stored energy.

3 _______________ depends on the position of an object relative to Earth.

4 _______________ is the energy of a stretched rubber band or a compressed spring.

5 _______________ is the energy due to motion.

**3** **Mark (✓) the correct sentences. Correct the other sentences.**

1 Gravitational potential energy depends on how high an object is.

2 Energy ~~can~~ *cannot* change the motion of an object, its temperature or other characteristics.

3 Elastic potential energy stops a pole-vaulter from jumping too high.

4 An object does not need to be moving to have energy.

5 The bigger an object is, the less kinetic energy it has.

**4** **Describe the energy shown in the photos. Read and write. You can use words more than once.**

mechanical    elastic potential
kinetic    destroyed    transferred
gravitational potential



> **Grammar Tip**
>
> When a carpenter swings a hammer **slowly**, the hammer has a small amount of kinetic energy.
>
> When a carpenter swings a hammer **quickly**, it has more kinetic energy, and can push a nail farther.

**1** As we wind up the toy, the springs inside it gain ___elastic potential___ energy. As the springs unwind, the ________________ energy is transformed into ________________ energy.

**2** At this point, the soccer ball has ________________ energy. Part of it comes from the ________________ energy of its motion, and part of it comes from the ________________ energy stored in it due to its high position.

**3** When dead organic matter decomposes, the chemical energy stored in it is not ________________. It is ________________ into the new matter that is formed—for example, coal.

**5** **Complete the sentences, using the adverbial form of the adjective in parentheses.**

**1** An object that has a lot of elastic potential energy moves more ___quickly___. (quick)

**2** Rubber bands stretch more ____________ at higher temperatures. (easy)

**3** A lightning bug shines more ____________ in the dark. (bright)

**4** When the wind speed is low, the windmill moves ____________. (slow)

**6** **How do you use energy? In your notebook, write answers to the questions.**

**1** How do you use gravitational potential energy? Give an example.

**2** In which situations does elastic potential energy help you in your everyday life?

**3** How do you use mechanical energy? Give an example.

# Lesson 2 · What is sound energy?

**1** What is sound energy? Circle *a*, *b*, or *c*.

**1** Sound is ______________ spreads from its source.

  **a** the direction in which energy     **b** a wave of vibrations that     **c** the navigation of energy that

**2** A ______________ wave is created when vibrating objects transmit energy through the air.

  **a** sound     **b** source     **c** vocal

**3** A vacuum is empty space with no ______________.

  **a** soundproof     **b** energy     **c** particles

**4** ______________ is a measure of how often particles are vibrating.

  **a** The number of particles in a wave     **b** Sound     **c** Frequency

**5** Humpback whales use vocalization to ______________.

  **a** locate and identify objects     **b** communicate     **c** navigate

**6** Echolocation is the use of sound to ______________.

  **a** communicate     **b** send out calls     **c** locate and identify objects

**2** Look at the photos. Read and match.

___ **a** It increases or decreases the sound volume.

___ **b** It makes a high-pitched sound.

___ **c** It makes a low-pitched sound.

___ **d** It uses echolocation.

**3** What happens when you sing? Read and write.
There is one extra word.

> sound    frequency    low-pitched
> echolocation    high-pitched    ~~vocalization~~
> sound waves    volume

**Hear me sing! By Martin Newman**

What I do when I sing is a kind of **(1)** _vocalization_. Here's how it happens. The energy of the air that comes from my lungs causes my vocal cords to vibrate. The energy of the vibrations is transferred through the air in the form of **(2)** ________________. When the energy of the original vibrations reaches your ears, it makes your eardrums vibrate, too, and you hear **(3)** ______________, that is, you hear me sing.

I can increase the **(4)** ______________ of the sound I make. To do that, I push air out of my lungs with more force. The increased energy makes your eardrums vibrate more, and you hear a louder sound.

I am 11 years old. The **(5)** ______________ with which my vocal cords vibrate is high, so the sound of my voice is **(6)** ______________. When I'm older, my vocal cords will become thicker and longer, so they will vibrate more slowly, and the sound of my voice will be **(7)** ______________.

**4** Write comparative phrases, using the words in parentheses.

**1** _The lower the frequency, the lower the pitch_ of the sound will be. (low/ frequency, low/pitch)

**2** ______________________________ of the sound will be. (small/object, high/pitch)

**3** ______________________________ to the sound source, ______________________________ will be. (close/you are, loud/sound)

**5** Your own voice. In your notebook, write answers to the questions.

**1** When might you need to increase the volume of your voice? How do you do it?

**2** What happens when you speak in a room that's completely empty? Why?

**3** Is your voice high-pitched or low-pitched? Why?

**1** Light can pass through some materials and not others. Write the missing letters.

The curtain is
_o_ _p_ a _g_ _u_ e.

The lamp shade is
t r __ __ s l __ c __ n t.

The window pane is
t __ a n __ p __ __ __ n __.

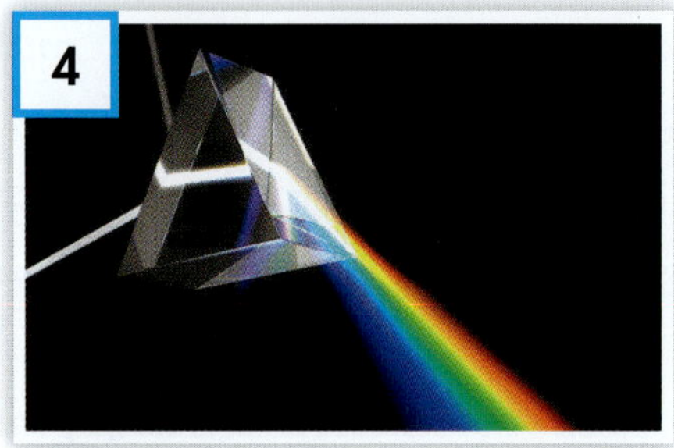

This picture shows
d __ __ p __ __ s i o n.

This picture shows
r __ f r __ c t __ __ n.

This picture shows
r __ __ l e __ t __ __ n.

**2** Read and write words from **1**.

**1** _Transparent_ materials let nearly all light pass through them.

**2** Light _____________ happens when white light is refracted and colors separate.

**3** Light _____________ happens when light enters a new material at an angle different from 90°.

**4** _____________ materials do not let any light pass through them.

**5** _____________ materials let some light pass through them.

**6** Light _____________ happens when light bounces off an object and goes in a different direction.

**3**    **Complete with *and*, *but*, or *or*.**

**1**   To protect yourself from ultraviolet radiation, you should stay away from the sun ______*or*______ wear sunscreen if you have to be in the sun.

**2**   X-rays have short wavelengths, ____________ radio waves have longer ones.



**3**   The colors of visible light mix ____________ produce white light.

**4**   A mirage makes you think there's water on a smooth surface in the distance, ____________, when you go near, there isn't any.

**5**   To explain color dispersion, you can use a prism ____________ a photo of a rainbow.

**4**    **Join the sentences, using the words in parentheses.**

**1**   Ultraviolet radiation is found in sunlight. We cannot see ultraviolet radiation. (but)
   *Ultraviolet radiation is found in sunlight, but we cannot see it.*

**2**   Microwaves heat up the water in food. Microwaves cook the food. (and)

**3**   You can't see ultraviolet light. You can't see infrared light. (or)

**4**   Light can go through translucent materials. Light can't go through opaque materials. (but)

**5**   You can see your reflection on a smooth surface made of glass. You can see it on a smooth surface made of metal. (or)

**5**    **Think about different forms of light energy that you use in your life. In your notebook, describe these different forms of light energy, and what you use them for.**

**1** Do the quiz. Circle *a*, *b* or *c*.

**1** On a very cold day, ＿ forms on windows when it's very warm inside the house.
- **a** evaporation
- **b** condensation
- **c** matter

**2** When you mix lemon juice, sugar, and water, sugar is the ＿.
- **a** solute
- **b** solvent
- **c** solution

**3** Burning something causes a ＿.
- **a** melting point
- **b** chemical change
- **c** different substance

**4** ＿ is a type of friction.
- **a** Gravity
- **b** Motion
- **c** Air resistance

**5** When two opposite forces are ＿, the object they act on won't move.
- **a** magnetic
- **b** balanced
- **c** contact

**6** The force that a simple machine supplies is called the ＿.
- **a** output force
- **b** effort
- **c** input force

**7** Inside a battery, chemical energy is ＿ into electrical energy.
- **a** transformed
- **b** transferred
- **c** dispersed

**8** The higher an object is, the more ＿ potential energy it has.
- **a** mechanical
- **b** elastic
- **c** gravitational

**9** When particles vibrate very fast, the ＿ of the sound is high.
- **a** energy
- **b** reflection
- **c** pitch

**10** A ＿ material lets some light go through but not all.
- **a** transparent
- **b** translucent
- **c** visible

You get one point for each correct answer. What's your score?

**1–3** Oh dear!   **4–5** OK.   **6–8** Very good!   **9–10** Excellent!

The hidden word is: ________________

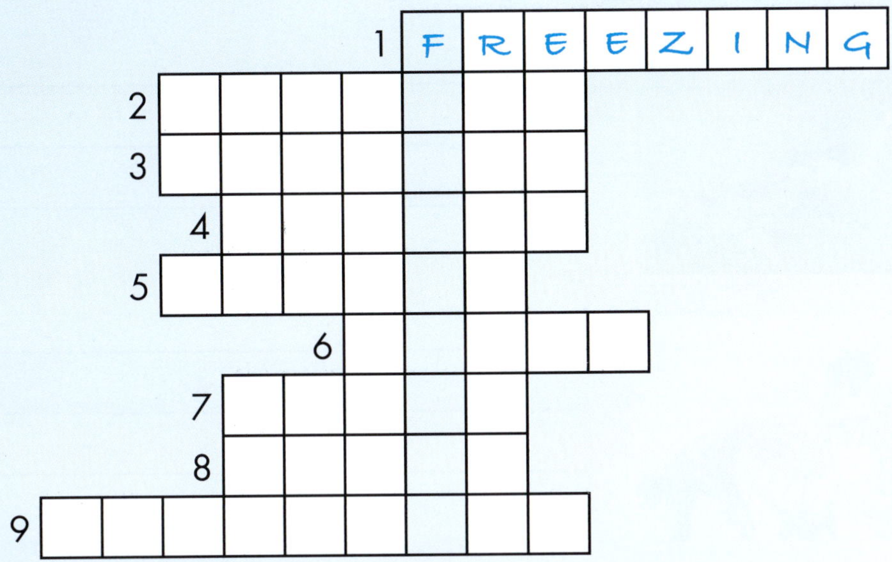

**1** The ENEZGRIF point of water is 0 °C. _FREEZING_

**2** A lever moves around a UFRCMUL. ________________

**3** Water is called a "universal OVLTNSE". ________________

**4** You can't see through PEUOQA material. ________________

**5** Sound cannot travel in a MUVAUC. ________________

**6** A GEEWD is a simple machine. ________________

**7** Vibrating objects can produce OSDNU waves. ________________

**8** A system of pulleys reduces the amount of input OCERF needed. ________________

**9** Energy cannot be made or ODEESRYDT. ________________

**3** **Can you find two sentences with incorrect information? Correct them.**

**1** We cannot see ultraviolet light.

**2** A simple machine is made up of two or more parts.

**3** A liquid has a definite volume but no definite shape.

**4** A mirage is a result of the dispersion of light.

# Vocabulary

**Which words do you want to remember? Write.**

**Unit 1**

**Unit 2**

**Unit 3**

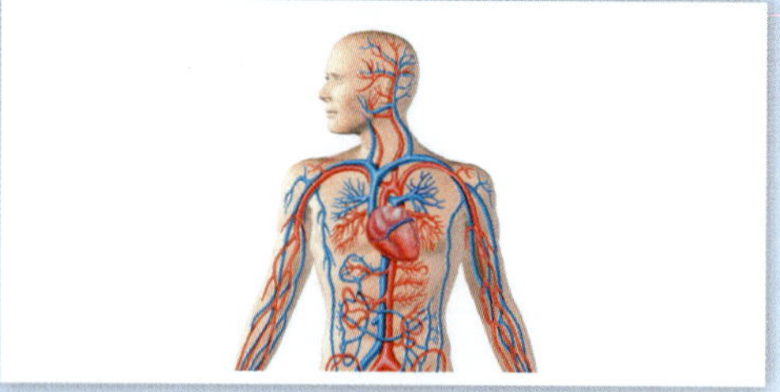

**Unit 4**

**Unit 5**

**Unit 6**

**Unit 7**  ________________________________

________________________________

________________________________

**Unit 8**  ________________________________

________________________________

________________________________

**Unit 9**  ________________________________

________________________________

________________________________

**I can read and write words about...**

| | | ✓ | ✗ |
|---|---|---|---|
| **Unit 1** | design and function | ☐ | ☐ |
| **Unit 2** | survival and extinction | ☐ | ☐ |
| **Unit 3** | body systems and function | ☐ | ☐ |
| **Unit 4** | water and weather | ☐ | ☐ |
| **Unit 5** | Earth's surface | ☐ | ☐ |
| **Unit 6** | Earth and space | ☐ | ☐ |
| **Unit 7** | matter | ☐ | ☐ |
| **Unit 8** | forces and motion | ☐ | ☐ |
| **Unit 9** | energy | ☐ | ☐ |

# Reading Skills

## Units 1–5 · What do I know?

**Unit 1**  **I can replace words in a text to avoid repetition.**

Replace the underlined words with the correct pronoun.

> The engineer builds a prototype of her design solution and then (**1**) the engineer tests (**2**) the prototype to ensure that the solution works. While testing, the engineer must take careful measurements and record (**3**) the measurements in a log.

**Unit 2**  **I can find specific information in a text.**

Go to page 18 of the Student's Book. Read the text with the title *Life Cycle Variations*. Answer these questions.

**1** When do birds lay their eggs? _______________________________

**2** Why? _______________________________

**Unit 3**  **I can identify the main points in a text.**

Go to page 37 of the Student's Book. Read the text with the title *Involuntary Actions*. Write the main points.

**1** _______________________________

**2** _______________________________

**3** _______________________________

**Unit 4**  **I can identify the topics of different paragraphs in a text.**

Go to page 42 of the Student's Book. Read the text with the title *Barometric Pressure*. What is the topic?

_______________________________

**Unit 5**  **I can understand the main idea of a text, even if I don't know all the words.**

Go to page 59 of the Student's Book. Read the text with the title *Fossil Fuels*. Answer the questions.

**1** What fossil fuel does it focus on? _______________________________

**2** When you first read the text, what were the words that you didn't know?

_______________________________

**3** Did it stop you from understanding the text? _______________________________

# Units 6–9 · What do I know?

**Unit 6**  **I can extract specific information from a text by searching for key words.**

Go to page 72 of the Student's Book. Read the text with the title *Dwarf Planets*. Answer the question.

Who discovered Pluto?

_______________________________________________

**Unit 7**  **I can guess the meaning of a word I don't know by looking at the words around it.**

What does *sediment* mean? Read and guess.

*A glass contained salt water. The water has evaporated, leaving white <u>sediment</u> behind.*

_______________________________________________

**Unit 8**  **I can follow the logical connection of sentences in a text.**

Read and underline the word that connects the two parts of this sentence. What is the connection between the sentences? Mark (✓) the correct option.

*An object begins to move because a force has acted on it.*

**1** The first half of the sentence gives the reason for the second half of the sentence.

**2** The second half of the sentence gives the reason for the first half of the sentence

**Unit 9**  **I can follow the sequence of events to understand how a process happens.**

Read and put the sentences in the correct order.

**a** For example, when a pole vaulter's pole bends, elastic potential energy increases.

**b** This type of potential energy is present when things are bent or stretched.

**c** The more a rubber band is stretched, the more elastic potential energy it has.

**d** Elastic potential energy is the energy of a stretched rubber band.

# Writing Skills

**Unit 1**  **I can write questions to find out more information about a topic.**

Read the blog. Write three questions to find out more information.



1 _______________________________________________________________

2 _______________________________________________________________

3 _______________________________________________________________

**Unit 2**  **I can give factual information, using the present passive.**

Read the factfile. Write the present passive form of the verbs.

force    form    use    cover    produce

Coal (**1**) _______________ when plants and trees die and they (**2**) _______________ with water and mud. As more plants die, more layers of plant matter (**3**) _______________. Over time, the oxygen within the layers (**4**) _______________ out. The coal that remains (**5**) _______________ to produce electricity.

**Unit 3**  **I can write advice on keeping healthy.**

Write some advice on how to keep the circulatory system working well.

1 _______________________________________________________________

2 _______________________________________________________________

3 _______________________________________________________________

**Unit 4**  **I can use the present perfect to ask questions.**

Think about different kinds of weather someone in another country may have experienced. Write three questions about the weather, using the present perfect.

1 _______________________________________________________________

2 _______________________________________________________________

3 _______________________________________________________________

**Unit 5**   **I can talk about the future of the environment.**

How can pollution harm the environment?
Write two sentences.

1  ______________________________________

   ______________________________________

2  ______________________________________

   ______________________________________

**Unit 6**   **I can compare different objects in space.**

Write two sentences comparing Earth and the sun.

1  ______________________________________

2  ______________________________________

**Unit 7**   **I can make suggestions, using *could*.**

Read the sentences. Then write suggestions, using *could*.

1  I'd like to make a solid dissolve in a liquid faster.

   ______________________________________

2  My lemonade isn't cold enough.

   ______________________________________

**Unit 8**   **I can label a picture.**

Look at the photo of the complex machine.
Label the different simple machines it is
made of. Complete the sentence.

This ______________ can be used for

______________________________.

**Unit 9**   **I can write descriptions using adverbs.**

Write descriptive sentences using these adverbs.

1  quickly: ______________________________

2  brightly: _____________________________

# Study Skills

## Carrying out an investigation

- Think about the topic you want to find out about.

- Reflect on what you already know. How can you build your understanding of the topic?

- Consider the different kinds of questions you can ask:

| What | is | … | ? |
|---|---|---|---|
| Where | are | … | ? |
| When | do | … | ? |
| Why | does | … | ? |
| How | can | … | ? |
| How long | … | | ? |
| How much | … | | ? |
| How many | … | | ? |
| How often | … | | ? |
| Can a | … | | ? |
| Does a | … | | ? |
| Has a | … | | ? |
| Is a | … | | ? |
| Are | … | | ? |
| Will a | … | | ? |

- Think about how you are going to carry out your investigation. What is your method? Why have you chosen it? Are you going to do it once only, or are you going to repeat it?

- Decide how you are going to record your results. Are you going to write notes, or complete a table or a chart? Are you going to draw pictures or diagrams, or take photographs?

## Examining your results

- Look at the detail of your results. Can you find any patterns? Is there anything unexpected?

- Investigate similarities and differences in your results.

- Consider reasons for what you find in your results.

- Sort or classify the results into different groups, using graphs, charts, and diagrams. Does this help you understand more about your results?

- Decide how your results fit with what you already know about the topic.

## Communicating your findings

- Reflect on who you want to communicate your findings to. What will be the best way to communicate with them?

- Think about the different tools you can use, and how you can combine words and pictures to present your findings.

- Consider the sequence in which you will present your findings.

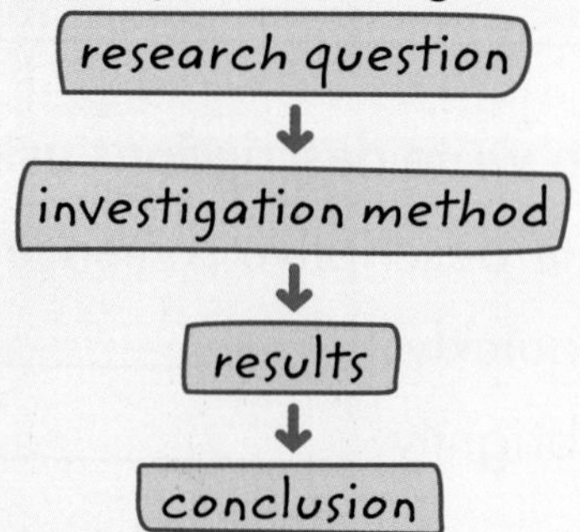


- Explain what you have learned from your investigation. Is there anything you want to find out more about?